T0194951

THE EMERALD-GREEN
and BLACK DAMSELFLY

One Patient's Journey through COVID-19

ISABELLE K. JEAN

WESTBOW
PRESS®
A DIVISION OF THOMAS NELSON
& ZONDERVAN

WestBow Press books may be ordered through booksellers or by contacting:

WestBow Press
A Division of Thomas Nelson & Zondervan
1663 Liberty Drive
Bloomington, IN 47403
www.westbowpress.com
844-714-3454

ISBN: 978-1-6642-3980-7 (sc)
ISBN: 978-1-6642-3981-4 (hc)
ISBN: 978-1-6642-3979-1 (e)

Library of Congress Control Number: 2021913684

Print information available on the last page.

WestBow Press rev. date: 08/10/2021

CONTENTS

A special thank-you to all my amazing family, friends,
and special people who prayed
for me and helped me through
this journey. I will never
forget your
acts of kindness.

Each chapter closes with a Bible verse and a simple thought to
help you live life large, with a sense of God's purpose.

> Ah, Sovereign Lord, you have made the heavens and
> the earth by your great power and outstretched arm.
> Nothing is too hard for you.
>
> —Jeremiah 32:17

INTRODUCTION

My purpose in writing this book is to help those who are taking the same journey know they're not alone. It's to help those fortunate enough to avoid this journey gain perspective on the path we COVID-19 patients have trod.

My journey began on a Saturday afternoon, no different from any other Saturday in our twenty-five years of marriage. My husband, James, came back from golfing with his foursome, but he was more than just the normal tired after logging about twelve thousand steps on the course and getting up at the crack of dawn; he didn't feel quite right. As the evening wore on, he developed a fever and became sicker with each passing hour. He received a COVID-19 test in the emergency room at our local hospital because he had some of the symptoms that news anchors reported. The doctor told him to go home and take pain relievers, and they would notify him of his results. By Sunday, he was no better; still had a fever and felt miserable—so miserable that he told me to go outside and breathe fresh air so I didn't get sick. Little did he or I know that I and one of his golfing buddies would be diagnosed with COVID-19 within a few days.

We recently had moved to Maryland's eastern shore, and one of my favorite spots to visit was a national wildlife refuge. I drove there for fresh air. Because of COVID-19, the refuge waived entrance fees, and you could drive through any time of the day or evening and observe the wildlife and marshy areas. It was an oasis to me whenever

I visited. An observation pier was constructed to allow you to become a part of the marsh. At the end of the pier, there are two telescopes near an iron bench, where you can sit to observe the bald eagles or any other birds, wildlife, insects, or waterfowl that call this place home. It is a quiet place, a place I discovered to get close to God. Praying there is easy to do, and on that day, I felt so close to God that I didn't know where I ended and He began. It was a beautiful sunny day in mid-August, and I felt His peace surrounding me at the end of that pier.

A distant osprey's cry and water trickling in through the marsh as the tide flowed were the only two sounds. I began to pray. "I have three prayers that I want to bring before You, God." First, I prayed for my relationship with my husband. Raising children, pursuing a career, participating in church activities, entertaining friends, taking care of pets, traveling, and so many other things had taken precedence over our relationship. None of these pastimes was bad, but I knew he needed to be elevated to the place where he belonged, directly under my relationship with God.

The second prayer concerned our dog, Max. We had adopted him about five years ago, and he had become an idol to me. I catered to his every whim; he slept in his own Sleep Number bed in the guest room (for those of you who can relate, his number is 100), and he ate dog food from Canada that was approximately a hundred dollars a bag. I took him outside for walks every two to three hours so he would be comfortable, and I could never go too far myself because I had to let Max out. Just talk to James, and he'll tell you that he, most assuredly, took a back seat to "Mr. Max."

I said, "God, I've made a mistake in my priorities. You can take the dog if that's what's required to help me remove the idol status attached to him." This was a huge offering on my part. I knew when I said it how Abraham felt when he was willing to give up his son Isaac in the wilderness in Genesis 22:9–12 (to a slightly lesser degree, for all non-dog lovers who are reading this and saying, "Really?").

A serious desire to be used by God was my final prayer request.

I said, "I want to be Your eyes, Your ears, and Your heart to a lost and dying world. When people look at me, I want them to see You so clearly that there is no question to whom I belong. I want to help others find the peace I have come to know through You so that they too will find joy for their journey. Please guide and direct me to people who need You."

I didn't feel or see the emerald-green and black damselfly that landed on my hot-pink T-shirt squarely on my stomach because I was totally focused on my quiet time with God. When I opened my eyes, it was shimmering in the sunlight and was the most beautiful shade of green, more brilliant than any emerald stone I had ever seen in a store's jewelry case. There was black interspersed on its long abdomen. Then I looked at its wings. They were intricately designed and looked like finely woven lace. Its big yellow eyes were looking at me, and it was turning its head back and forth about 180 degrees. I said, "God, I have never seen such a creature, and I can't believe that you designed something that beautiful." It was such a gift to be able to see this insect, and I thanked God for eyes to see and a heart to appreciate His workmanship. I reached for my cell phone to take its picture, knowing that no one would believe the colors and wing patterns if I tried to describe them. My shirt moved, and it flew away. I felt honored and grateful that it had landed on me; I thanked God that He cared enough about us to design something that amazing for us to observe.

And that is how this book was named. On that day, I had no idea I was already infected with COVID-19 and that my trip to the refuge was the beginning of my journey with a disease that I would later call "the Beast."

> What other nation is so great as to have their gods near
> them the way the Lord our God is near us whenever
> we pray to Him? (Deuteronomy 4:7)

Live life large. When I am in the lowest valleys, I have seen the highest degree of work done by God.

HOSPITALS

THE COVID-19 SYMPTOMS I EXPERIENCED BECAME increasingly less each passing day. I battled a fever for seven days, had no appetite, no sense of smell or taste, not enough fluid intake, and no sleep. I was rapidly losing weight and strength. Just when I thought the disease had run its course, I started feeling faint and dizzy. I got up in the middle of the night, and as I tried to get back into bed, I passed out. My dog, Max, was standing over me, licking my face, when I regained consciousness. I was quite shocked to find myself with a serious rug burn on my face and severe pain in my shoulder from the fall; I didn't remember anything. James and I were quarantined and sleeping in separate rooms, so I had to call him to help me get back into bed. I grew weaker as the night progressed and asked him to call 911 in the morning. He told the emergency medical services (EMS) workers that we both had COVID-19, so they took the proper precautions. They took all my vital signs, including my oxygen levels, and said that while they could take me to the hospital if I insisted, the protocol they were following was to let COVID-19 patients recover at home. They said, "Drink more fluids and eat something."

I promised them I would try because I didn't want to go to the hospital—I just wanted reassurance that I wasn't dying. They assured me that it was dehydration-related, but within two days, I was weaker, couldn't eat anything at all, and breathing was difficult.

A friend who had helped me in the past with zero balancing—a hands-on healing modality that facilitates structural balance and stronger flows of energy in the body—said she'd been successful in performing her gift remotely, due to the pandemic. We prayed together, and I asked for her help. She prayed that God would help me use every ounce of energy I could possibly find within my body to heal from COVID-19. She said she had a word from God after she prayed, and He said, "She is already healed." I remembered and leaned on those words many times throughout my hospital stay.

My oxygen level was in the low nineties and dropping when we checked the oximeter. Family members and nurse friends said we had to call EMS again, and this time, I should go to the hospital; I went. My breathing was labored, I was losing more weight, and I was severely dehydrated now. I knew I could get fluids and oxygen in the hospital and knew I needed help. There was so much prayer from so many people that I could feel the presence of God surrounding me. I reached up with my right hand many times from that point on to ask Jesus to hold my hand. He never failed to do so. I remembered the Bible verse, "For I am the Lord, your God, who takes hold of your right hand and says to you, Do not fear; I will help you" (Isaiah 41:13).

When the EMS workers showed up, I was weak and had difficulty speaking. As I struggled to answer their questions, I was interrupted by a loud, cell phone ringtone; one of my favorite singer's (Kane Brown) song. The EMS worker forgot to mute his cell phone, and I had to wait until he was able to silence his phone to continue telling them my symptoms.

After I was recovering back home, I called the county EMS office and shared my experience. I hoped no one worse off than me would have to talk over Kane Brown's singing. They were grateful for the feedback, and they used it as a teaching moment for all of their teams.

"Acute respiratory distress syndrome (ARDS) due to COVID-19

virus" was my formal medical diagnosis. I don't believe our small local hospital was prepared to handle such a case. However, "let nothing be wasted" (John 6:12); I learned a valuable lesson in patience that day.

A doctor at the Johns Hopkins Hospital (JHH), a family member, texted me after I'd spent several hours in our local hospital. James had contacted him with details of my medical condition, and he said, "You need to be transported as soon as possible to Baltimore to be seen by doctors at the JHH."

I agreed. Almost eleven hours after I arrived in our local hospital emergency room and was transferred to an Intensive Care Unit room, I was released to be transported to the JHH. During my healing process, I was able to meet with the president and CEO of the medical center to discuss some shortfalls I had found in his facility. He used the input as a training experience to help others who are sure to come after me on this journey.

When I requested a meeting with the president of the Shore Regional Health, I quoted from the Focus on the Family website:

> Christians and Lawsuits: God is honored when disciples of Christ who earnestly desire to seek His will sit down together and work out their differences in a peaceful and respectful manner.

I believe that this was handled as such on both sides of the table.

We had quite a ride from the shore to Baltimore that night. My transport attendant knelt down by my bedside when we first met and said, "I don't know what strings you pulled to get into the JHH, but I want you to be prepared for a rough ride. We have construction ahead of us, light rail tracks, and a lot of bumps."

He had no way of knowing about the hour-long traffic jam we would encounter due to clearing an attempted suicide on the Bay Bridge. As we sat at a standstill, I prayed for those involved, for those who had no hope.

At the JHH Division of Infectious Diseases Unit, I was impressed with the nurse assigned to my room. She was compassionate, caring, and very efficient at her task of moving me from the gurney to my bed. When she rolled me over to transfer beds, I couldn't breathe, and I thought I was going to die. She handled it professionally, and after I reached for Jesus's hand and prayed, I was able to calm down and stop the panic attack. She wore a respirator on her back, a clear shield on her face, another mask on her face, a gown from neck to shins, and two pairs of gloves (which, I later learned from the nurses, greatly limited manual dexterity) for protection; this was standard protocol for anyone entering my room for the next six days.

Within the first few hours of my arriving at the JHH, the nurse informed me that *pronation* (lying flat on your stomach) was the preferred method of recovery. We have a pharmacist in our family who gave me that advice before I was in the hospital, and I was grateful for the confirmation. Only a loving God could design us so that the lungs function with the least resistance when they rest in the chest cavity. I am prone to vertigo, and every time I turned over for vital statistics or blood work, vertigo symptoms started. I prayed that God would spare me from the spinning sensation, on top of ARDS and COVID-19. It usually lasted less than a minute each time it happened.

I hadn't eaten for twenty-four hours. In the morning, when breakfast arrived, I took the lid off the plate to discover a *God-wink*; that's something God does that blesses you and lets you know that "He sees you, He knows you, He loves you" (words from Twila Paris's song, "Every Heart That Is Breaking"). James jokes with me because *every time* we go to breakfast at Cracker Barrel, I always order the same meal—a scrambled egg, one piece of bacon, a bran muffin, and a cup of coffee. There, under the lid, was that exact meal. It made me smile, and I thanked God for His watchful care.

The nurse said patients who recovered the quickest exercised their lungs using a spirometer (on which I received training within an hour of entering the JHH). I had used a spirometer some years ago after a fall, so I wasn't new to this exercise. However, when I tried to take a slow, deep breath to expand and fill my lungs with air, I could barely get fifty milliliters of air into my lungs. By the end of my six days in the JHH, after breathing with the spirometer many times a day, I was able to achieve volumes of 1,500–2,000 milliliters, which, I believe, was instrumental to my recovery. My ninety-two-year-old mother uses a spirometer daily, performing six breaths each session, several times a day. She called me every day while I was hospitalized, and what I remember most was her strong voice. I attribute this to her daily lung exercises and can't stress enough the value of this instrument. They cost less than ten dollars and are very easy to operate.

The doctors' and nurses' floor-length protective gowns were donated by Ford Motor Corporation "to help further protect health care workers. Ford is leading efforts to manufacture reusable gowns from airbag materials with supplier Joyson Safety Systems" (as noted on the Ford website, where I learned they also are producing respirators, masks, and other items for medical use). The doctors and nurses go through so many outfit changes between rooms that the biohazard container in my room filled up constantly. One of the nurses and I praised Ford Motor Corporation for helping the environment with their recycling mission and for stepping up to do something positive for this pandemic.

I remember my second night at the JHH, when I realized I had nothing but my cell phone, my wallet, and the pajamas that I'd worn from home. I quickly became a minimalist and got by for the next six days with the toothpaste, toothbrush, soap, and shampoo provided by the hospital. I would recommend everyone pack a small bag with daily essentials and put it in a closet to take with you, should you ever need to go to the hospital.

In the early evening, I received a text from a dear friend with some comforting words, quoted from Patsy Clairmont: "Breathe, another day is tucked in for the night." That meant so much to me that I reread it several times, into the early morning hours. She is the same friend who gave me a sign some time ago that reads, "Friends Are God's Way of Taking Care of Us," to which I wholeheartedly agree; so many friends reached out to me on this journey.

One day, I awoke suddenly and thought I was dying. When I opened my eyes, there were two nurses standing over me, and I felt like I was underwater. I could see the surface and bubbles, and they were in the light, but I couldn't breathe or get to the surface. I was having a very realistic panic attack and could hear them saying, "Breathe; you have oxygen," but I couldn't. They finally convinced me I had air, and after a minute or two, I calmed down and was able to breathe. It was the closest I have ever been to dying, and I don't want anyone to experience that type of death if I can help them. (There is a chapter on smoking and vaping in this book that stemmed from this experience.)

I played Christian music day and night on my cell phone. There are so many beautiful, meaningful songs and so many talented Christian artists publishing music today; I was so blessed by their songs and voices. I believe this played a huge role in my upbeat attitude and also added joy for the journey.

Family and friends wanted to visit me in the hospital or at least send in some fresh clothes or simple things that I needed, but they were unable to do so in the Infectious Diseases Unit. I was told the only items that were allowed to be sent in were electronics. There were a few things I wanted badly but one thing that stands out the most was dental floss. I floss my teeth regularly, but with COVID-19 symptoms, I had been too sick and weak to floss. After spending a few days in the hospital, I was feeling a bit better, had eaten some food, and realized I hadn't flossed my teeth for many days. I asked for dental floss but was told they had none in stock. So, in my sleepless and bored condition, this became a focal point to me—how to floss my teeth.

I started thinking of how to improvise. I looked at my blanket;

it had a worn spot on it. Was there a string? Yes, but not long enough. I thought of my hair, but it was too short. I thought of my doctor's hair, as it was quite long, but I didn't have the nerve to ask her for a strand. It was then that a nurse came in to check my vital statistics, and when she stood in the light of the door, I thought I finally had my answer. There, hanging on the bottom of her gown, were several strings. I told her this would probably be the only time in her life that a patient would ask for this but, if at all possible, would she pull off one of those strings and let me use it as dental floss?

She looked at me to see if I was kidding and said, "Are you serious? No, that is really dirty." She did laugh, and I decided I had stooped pretty low at that point. I was satisfied to just wait until it came in.

It finally came in on the day I was discharged; my doctor and I joked that it was probably twenty-five dollars for the little box. On my last day in the hospital, I told the doctor I had received the dental floss, and she said, "Is it mint?" That made me laugh because I didn't care what flavor it was, as long as I got the food accumulation out of my teeth. Ah, the simple pleasures of life! (Pack dental floss in your small bag to take with you if you suddenly have to go to the hospital.)

One of the amazing administrative staff in the hospital ordered for me, along with that delightful box of dental floss (and it was mint-flavored after all), powder-blue, non-slip socks; white sweatpants; a white sweatshirt; and a white T-shirt for my journey home. I couldn't wait for the ensemble to come in and checked on its status often. Finally, on the day of my discharge, the administrative staff member came in with my going-home outfit. He had the most beautiful smile (as I told him), and you can't believe how happy I was to see him walk into my room, outfit in hand.

I got dressed for the first time in several weeks. It was a long process because I had to rest between putting on each item of clothing. When he came back into the room, he said I looked like I was "going on a cruise." I had my socks on and my white outfit, with my sweatshirt tied around my neck. He smiled from ear to ear. He knew he had made a patient very happy, and it showed all over his face. There is a special section about him in the chapter titled "Nurses, Nurses' Assistants, and Administrative Staff," and he holds a special place in my heart.

I was afraid to leave the hospital. The JHH is the "Ritz-Carlton" of hospitals, and I couldn't have been in better hands. The quality and efficiency of the hospital staff, the delicious food (the salmon and sweet potato were my favorites), and the comfortable room would all be missed. I knew that I would leave behind the twenty-four-hour monitoring of my vital statistics when I was discharged. It was comforting, knowing how well I was cared for, and I wasn't sure I was ready to leave that comfort level.

Two days before discharge, my potassium levels were inconsistent, and the doctors were concerned about my heart functions. Late one night, a phlebotomist came in to draw blood, and I wondered, *How will this work when I am at home?* My heart function turned out OK but still left me slightly afraid of leaving behind the expertise and excellent medical support within a day or two.

My husband and I had COVID-19 at the same time, and he was still recuperating, weak, and exhausted. He couldn't make the trip to Baltimore to drive me home; we had no idea how I would get there. Then the Occupational Health nurse told me about a free-ride program for COVID-19 patients (paid for by a wealthy contributor). Several Yellow Cabs had been retrofitted with plexiglass and plastic wrap to ensure that no germs were passed from the back seat to the front. One of those cabs would take me home. I told the nurse I lived about ninety miles from the JHH, and she said, "That's OK; it's covered."

On the day I was discharged, the cab pulled up and drove me home that evening. My driver was amazing and couldn't have been nicer. He put his life on the line, not knowing if I was still infectious. He just cared enough to get me home to recover. The ride home was traffic free, and the trip over the Bay Bridge was more beautiful than I ever remember it. The sun was shining on the water, ships were coming and going, and life was, well, normal.

I was still very weak and frightened about going home, but I knew that was the best place for me to get well. God hadn't left me alone in the hospital. He promised to never leave me, so I figured I would be OK at home. On the ride home, I praised God for wealthy people who donated their money to ease the anxiety of others and for cab drivers who carried out the blessing.

I'd been home for a few days when I received a survey from the JHH. After praising them for every aspect of my stay, I made a couple of suggestions. My first suggestion was that the hospital should provide pads for patients' elbows and knees on the first day of their stays to avoid bedsores. My cousin told me that her father had to hold himself up on the side railings of the bed to relieve the stinging of skin rubbed raw by being bedridden. My heart ached for him, as I knew how he felt—my knees and elbows were raw skin when I left.

The second suggestion was that the JHH should purchase massage tables for ARDS/COVID-19 patients so the patients' necks didn't become sore from pronation. From about day two, my neck was so sore that I couldn't get comfortable for the sixteen to eighteen hours they recommended in the prone position. Massage tables have a hole for the patient's face and would allow for a much more suitable body position. The nurses gave me a neck pillow, which helped.

Later in the book, I will discuss the mania symptoms I had, resulting from lack of sleep from the drug dexamethasone, but I think patients should be warned that this could happen to them so they and their families prepare for this condition.

ISABELLE K. JEAN -

Have I not commanded you? Be strong and courageous. Do not be terrified; do not be discouraged, for the Lord you God will be with you wherever you go. (Joshua 1:9)

Live life large. In the darkest times and loneliest places, God is with you. Just ask Him to help you.

DOCTORS

Dr. Lavine, my favorite doctor and family member, practices pediatrics through the JHH. Through his advice, recommendation, and assistance, I was treated at that prestigious hospital in Baltimore, Maryland. I will be grateful to him always.

Dr. Newman found a room for me at the JHH and facilitated my transfer from our local hospital. On my first day in the hospital, he entered my room to meet me. I was grateful to be able to thank him for helping me. He was a kind, caring doctor and very informative. He offered two treatment choices for COVID-19. The first one was to administer platelets from a donor who had recovered from COVID-19. The donor blood would contain antibodies that would help my body fight the disease. He thoroughly discussed the ramifications of this treatment, but the major one was rejection of the platelets by my body. Dr. Newman also discussed a platelet-donation program, where I could "pay it forward" by donating my blood platelets for someone infected with the disease or donating them and freezing them in the event I became infected with the virus again.

The second treatment, remdesivir and dexamethasone (a corticosteroid), was used for patients, he said, toward the end of COVID-19. We agreed on that treatment plan. The steroid prevented sleep but was helpful as an anti-inflammatory. I would later experience the ramifications of the dexamethasone. Daily, I was also given an anticlotting injection. Three days after the first dose of the drugs, a doctor came into my room and said the medication had worked. When I told him how many people were praying for me, he said he figured that "a lot more was going on here." I never saw that doctor before or after his visit, but I remember he had beautiful blue eyes that sparkled as he delivered the prognosis of my healing.

I was able to text Dr. Newman through Dr. Levine, thanking him for his wonderful care. Here is his response:

> What a humbling statement. Please tell her I am thrilled she did so well and I wish her the best in her recovery. I thank her and I'll use her humbling encouragement as fuel in the service of the next patient.

The doctors at the JHH are rotated through the Infectious Diseases Unit for two-week stints. One morning, I was lying in bed when a young, energetic doctor entered my room. She and I began talking. The steroids had given me endless energy, and she caught me at a moment of brain excitability. We connected immediately and talked for a while about my disease.

She asked at one point, "Who are you? It's like you're in my head. You know what I'm going to say before I even say it." She stopped a moment and then said, "Are you a Leo?"

"Yes, my birthday is July 24," I told her.

"Mine is July 23," she said.

We high-fived on being the same sign and proceeded to talk at what seemed to be a hundred miles per hour. She was a brilliant doctor, and I am grateful that our paths crossed.

When I thank God for the many valuable lessons He taught me through this journey, I also thank Him for allowing me to meet Dr. Kim. She was born in Hong Kong, and both of her parents were doctors in her hometown. Her father was the first doctor in her area to be invited to Germany to bring magnetic resonance imaging (MRI) techniques to their town.

"Did your parents want you to be a doctor?" I asked.

"My father encouraged me, but my mother wasn't as enthralled with the idea." She enlightened me about being a doctor in Hong Kong. Her mother saw about eighty patients a day; about forty in the morning and forty in the afternoon. She wrote many prescriptions and never could have encouraged a doctor/patient relationship like Dr. Kim and I had developed. Her mother wanted her to "just be happy," but her mother didn't think that was possible by becoming a medical doctor.

Dr. Kim told me about two very sad stories that occurred in Hong Kong, both relating to doctors. The first was about a woman surgeon who, through no fault of her own, lost a patient during surgery. One of the patient's family members entered a room where the surgeon was having a meeting. The surgeon was sitting with her back to the door and didn't see the intruder. Within seconds, the family member wielded a machete and took the surgeon's life.

The second story was about a skilled hand surgeon who similarly had performed surgery, and it didn't go as planned. The patient's son came into the surgeon's office, and before anyone could stop him, the son cut off the doctor's hands.

These two incidents were senseless and horrible, and I was saddened to hear about the mental illness and anger that was displayed. Dr. Kim said that after the incident, the prominent hand doctor was able to train others in his delicate skill. We thanked God for beauty that came from ashes.

We also shared laughs. One morning, as Dr. Kim sat by my bedside, I noticed she had a bandage on her leg, and I asked about it.

She told me, "My family and I took a walk one evening. My son was riding his scooter, and he challenged me to try it. I thought I was younger than I am, so I got on the scooter—only to realize that I was going down a slight hill. I soon was going faster than I thought I could control, so I tried to stop by running the scooter into the grass. I stopped abruptly but fell off in the process and injured my leg."

We laughed about not acting our ages, and it reminded me of a funny story that I shared with her.

Many years ago, my children's father left me for a younger woman. I didn't want to admit it, but I told Dr. Kim that I thought I could compete with this younger woman. Shortly after he left, he asked to pick up the children after church one Sunday, and he was going to bring this young woman (who was very beautiful, fit, and—did I mention young?). That Sunday morning, I dressed for success and put on my tightest skirt and highest heels.

"At the appointed pick-up time," I told Dr. Kim, "I walked across the church parking lot to talk with them about the children, and that's when it happened. My skirt was so tight that my walking was impaired. My black patent high heels had beautiful big bows on the toes. My right heel got caught in my left toe bow, and I fell—*splat!*— right in front of them."

"When I got up, my pantyhose was torn, my knees were a mess, and I had learned a very hard lesson. Not only was I unable to compete with the young woman, but the adages 'Pride goeth before a fall' and 'Act your age' were driven home."

"I can picture that whole scenario in my mind," Dr. Kim said.

She and I both had belly-shaking laughs.

We talked about current events in our country and discussed race issues. I told her, "I want to say to the people who are rioting, 'I didn't do this to you. Maybe many generations ago, my relatives did this, but I didn't do anything to you.'" Then I told her that I was reading a book about slavery, *Narrative of the Life of Frederick Douglass, an American Slave*, which Douglass wrote.

She and I agreed that slavery was horrible; we hated that it happened, and we were so sorry, but we agreed that we couldn't change history.

Our discussion turned to Pandora's box. I said, "It seems as if Pandora's box has been opened, and all of these social issues are pouring out."

She, in her infinite wisdom, said, "What if we are all inside Pandora's box, and God is trying to show us a way to get out?"

Brilliant.

During my recovery, I attended a 2020 Maryland Prays rally in my town at which people of all faiths, colors, and creeds gathered at the local Harriet Tubman mural and worshipped the one true God. Some of the brothers from the Jewish faith blew shofars (ancient musical instruments made from rams' horns) and called for repentance. Many people from different Native American tribes spoke and shared prayers of forgiveness for the treatment of their peoples. Descendants of Harriet Tubman were honored.

In the rally handout material, Apostle Michele Perrera, Pastor of Woodlawn Christian Fellowship in Gwynn Oak, Maryland, wrote, "the only way to change the past is to look back, glean the good, review the hard places. In the present seek God, listen carefully to His voice, and execute His plan to heal the future."

We are climbing out of the box, Dr. Kim. The Maryland flag colors (red, yellow, black, and white) and the skin colors of the group that had gathered correlated. All are precious in His sight.

Dr. Kim's and my last discussion took place on the morning after the first COVID-19 patient (he was from Hong Kong) was reinfected with the disease. This made national news, and because I wasn't sleeping, I read the reports in the middle of the night.

Early the next morning, when Dr. Kim came into my room, I was ecstatic. I praised God for creating us with an immune system that worked as God had planned it to work. I had read in the BBC News Health section that a thirty-three-year-old man was infected with COVID-19 in late March, and then, several months later, reinfected while traveling in Europe. The news said it showed two different strains of the virus, but it stated, "Those infected develop an immune response as their bodies fight off the virus which helps to protect them against it returning." It discussed the innate immune response and the adaptive immune response, working together to make it so the "second infection would be milder than the first" (James Gallagher, *BBC News*, August 24, 2020).

I thought this was wonderful news and worthy of some of the country's top medical staff stating, "What a God we serve who could design an immune system like this—and it worked!" I told Dr. Kim that we needed to celebrate with a glass of champagne, but we decided it was too early in the morning. We were both impressed with God's creation of the human body and were happy to hear that news.

Dr. Kim discharged me the next day. I was sad that I wouldn't see her much longer; I had become quite fond of her and loved our talks. She pushed for me to get my provided oxygen level to zero so that I could leave the hospital.

I told her, "I'm going to write a book, and you will be included in a chapter."

"That would be helpful for other COVID-19 patients," she said, and then she added, "I won't forget you—and I want a signed copy of your book when it's published."

"Thank you, Dr. Kim, for helping me get well and being a big part of my journey."

> To another faith by the same Spirit, to another gifts of healing by that one Spirit. (1 Corinthians 12:9)

Live life large. Recognize, remember, and rejoice over the good that can come from bad when it's sifted through the loving hands of God.

NURSES, NURSES' ASSISTANTS, AND ADMINISTRATIVE STAFF

T HE NURSES AT THE JHH WERE PROFESSIONAL, KNOWLEDGEABLE, and kind. Throughout my stay, every nurse, nurses' assistant, and administrative staff who helped me was passionate about their jobs. I met the nurses and assistants on each shift because I couldn't sleep from the dexamethasone injections. I could feel the brain-excitability effect of the IV drip within minutes, and I talked incessantly at all hours of the day and night.

Late one evening, a nurse came into my room and shared that her little girl's father had been shot and killed about a year ago. She voiced concern about raising her little girl alone; I asked her if we could pray together.

Before we prayed, I shared my story about being in an abusive relationship with my first husband. I married young and realized I had made a mistake when the abuse began. He would hold me by my feet and pound my head against the floor until the tenant in the apartment unit below beat on her ceiling with her broom handle to try to stop his abuse. One such episode ended when he brought his heavy boot back to kick me in the kidneys after he dropped me on the floor, but, by the grace of God, he stopped, mid-kick, and left the apartment.

I told this nurse that I understood losing someone to a gunshot because I became a widow a few years after we were married. The abuse went on for some time, but he later met someone else and asked to end our marriage. He murdered this new woman shortly after we separated and fled to Pennsylvania. When he realized that he would go to jail for murder, he abruptly ended his own life with a fatal gunshot.

It was a difficult time, and it was someone close who died from a gunshot; I could relate. Because we shared a common bond, our prayer became more meaningful and real. I prayed for her safety and the safety of her daughter and that she could care for and provide for her.

I couldn't miss the opportunity to tell this young nurse, "Tell your daughter every day, 'You are smart, you are kind, and you are very important'"—I adapted that from the movie *The Help*. I tell both of my granddaughters this as often as I can. I want to prevent girls from making the same mistakes I did, and it's my desire to help children to be handled or touched only with respect.

In retrospect, I wish I would have committed the following verse to memory in my early childhood. It would have helped me in so many ways: "I praise you because I am fearfully and wonderfully made; your works are wonderful, I know that full well" (Psalm 139:14).

I prayed with everyone who entered my room and asked for a hedge of protection from the many germs that surrounded them throughout the Infectious Diseases Unit. I prayed that their family members would be spared from the viruses they encountered daily. Not one nurse or nurses' assistant turned down my offer to pray with them during the six days I spent in the JHH.

One person on the administrative staff rejected my offer to pray for him. He was personable and kind but said, "I don't need any prayer." As he left my room, I prayed for his safety but also prayed that he'd realize he needed prayer; his working conditions alone were enough to pray for grace and mercy.

Within the hour, he came back into the room, and we both talked at the same time. I said, "Oh, you must have realized that you should never turn down an offer from someone who wants to pray for you."

And he said, "I've come back to your room because I realized I made a mistake in turning down your offer to pray for me."

We both bowed our heads and prayed together. When we finished, I told him that his mother did a great job of raising him and for that, he should be thankful. He flashed his beautiful smile at me and left the room. He placed the order for my dental floss and beautiful white sweatpants and sweatshirt ensemble. I will never forget him, his smile, or his *humility* in coming back to my room for prayer.

I asked the nurse for a blanket toward the end of my hospital stay. Instead, an amazing nurse brought me hot packs that she applied to my back as I lay in the prone position. You have to love those nurses at the JHH; they really know how to show a girl a good time. In my mind, I was immediately transported to a massage table in a Ritz-Carlton Hotel, receiving a hot-stone massage. This nurse and I agreed that the current pandemic's toll had cost us human touch. In the JHH, all of the doors were closed immediately when someone entered or left my room. I heard no outside talking, and I had no idea who was in the room next to me or on the ward. I interacted with no one except the doctors, nurses, nurses' assistants, and occasional administrative staff. I suggested to her that it would be so wonderful if the nurses or assistants could include a few-minutes massage once a day; I thought it would satisfy that craving for human interaction I missed so much.

I met many nurses, nurses' assistants, and administrative staff during my hospital stay. They were all excellent and instrumental in my healing journey. I will remember all of them.

I thank my God every time I remember you. In all my prayers for all of you, I always pray with joy. (Philippians 1:3–4)

Live life large. God doesn't waste any of our life experiences. He can use them all to connect us with those who need us to feel their pain.

MANIC

I WAS DIAGNOSED WITH MANIA SHORTLY AFTER I LEFT THE hospital, but I believe I was manic before I was discharged. I was administered dexamethasone, a strong steroid, when I got to my local hospital emergency room and again every day for six days. I suffered from severe sleep deprivation in the hospital, and it worsened when I came home. Racing thoughts, sleeplessness, and a vivid imagination of talking with God were symptomatic behaviors of the psychosis. My ongoing conversation with "God" established me in a position to fix any problem I deemed my responsibility. The God I saw and talked with sat in a chair in my room, chewed gum, and conferred with me often. One night during this illness, he jokingly said he was leaving.

I said, "You can't leave. You said in Deuteronomy 31:6, 'Be strong and courageous. Do not be afraid or terrified because of them, for the Lord your God goes with you; he will never leave you nor forsake you.'"

As he walked away, he turned and said, "I was just kidding. I'm not going anywhere," and he sat back down in the chair and examined his fingernails. It frightens me now to see the depth of my illness; he was so vivid.

Mania also produced abundant self-confidence, excessive talking, and poor decision-making. The hospital chaplains contacted me one night, and I preached a sermon, prayed, and led them in hymns for about thirty minutes. They discussed the hospital choir and said they were delighted they had called on me. I thought, *I should be making calls for them*, and I almost volunteered to do so for the rest of my stay.

Family and friends would call for a quick update on my health. After an hour and a half of my excessive talking, they would try to get off the phone, but I had "just one more thing" to tell them. James would come in and beg me to hang up and let the "poor caller" go. One day, while James was working, I called his safety officer. I decided I could help their 1,300 employees with a better preparedness-and-precaution plan for COVID-19, and I wanted to share it. Much to James's chagrin, I kept the poor gentleman on the phone for three hours, but much to my satisfaction, it resulted in a robust preparedness plan, mass mailing, website update, and safety-meeting schedule, sealing my notion that I was God—or at least a person very close to God.

My I-can-fix-anything attitude and excessive talking, with no filter on my mouth, hurt very close family members too. I was out of control. Mania exacerbated a judgmental spirit that had dug deep roots into the soil of my soul. When God's light shone into that darkness and I grasped the damage that judgmental words had caused, I learned a lesson that I pray I will never forget.

I was not diagnosed with mania, however, until I made a very poor decision. It was another sleepless night, 3:00 a.m., and I was talking with my friend "God." He said that the house we had rented in Florida for the month of January every year through Vacation Rental By Owner (VRBO) was not large enough for us; we needed a bigger and better house. After all, I survived ARDS and COVID-19 and almost died, so I should rent something to celebrate that success. He said to open the VRBO application on my phone and find a new rental property. I agreed with him and searched for a pet-friendly house, close to the beach. And there it was—a mansion. I looked at all of the amenities—the location, the kitchen, the spaciousness, the beauty—and God and I agreed this was the one.

After putting in my credit card number, he said, "Push the 'Request to Book' button."

I said, "I am going to have to go against you on this one. James and I agreed, early in our marriage, that we would never spend more than one hundred dollars without discussing the purchase."

He said, "Oh, just book it. Tell him it is only a blip on the radar screen. As a matter of fact, you're going to buy James a new Tesla, a home in a prestigious neighborhood in North Myrtle Beach, and a custom golf cart. All he has to do is pick the colors for the car and the golf cart. Tell him it's Christmas morning."

I couldn't wait to tell James the news. When he woke up, I told him it was "Christmas morning." Sleepy-eyed and half awake, he was clueless. I told him I'd found a bigger and better house to rent in Florida, and I mentioned all of the other presents he would have by December 1.

He said, "I'm a simple man and don't need a different house. The one we've rented for the past couple of years suits me just fine." He laughed about the Tesla, new home, and golf cart and, as expected, asked, "From where do you think the money will come to pay for all of these things?"

"It's only a blip on the radar screen," I replied.

He shook his head in disbelief as he headed toward the door for coffee, but I was not to be discouraged. I opened the VRBO application and asked him if he wanted to see the mansion. I got my credit card information so I could add it before pushing the Request to Book button.

James was now more awake. "What are you doing?" he asked. "Stop! Do not add your credit card information and book that property!"

"Watch this," I said, as I typed in the card number, expiration date, and the code on the back of the card. "Bam!" I said as I pushed the Request to Book button—and the charge was made.

As the color drained from his face, he said in a controlled but angry voice, "I don't know what you just did, but I am going to Dunkin' Donuts to get coffee. When I get back, this better be fixed, or our relationship is in serious trouble!" As he left, he let the front door slam.

Uh-oh, I thought, *I'd better fix this*. I wasn't upset because I told myself I could always book the house closer to the vacation time; I was sure it would be available. I sent the owner of the house a quick email to say that I had been diagnosed with ARDS and COVID-19, and I made a mistake by renting his property. I then telephoned my credit card company and explained the problem in much detail to a very patient woman.

She said, "Yes, I see that this morning you charged $32,763 and a $250 booking fee for that property. But if you contact the owners, they might be able to remove the charge because my screen says the fee is pending."

The house we had earlier booked for thirty days was about the same price as the mansion for three days, and the mansion slept *twenty-three people.* I was shocked. I never looked at the daily cost or the number of people the home accommodated. It certainly exemplified poor decision-making.

I quickly opened my email account to contact the property owner and was surprised to see that he had emailed me a response. He said he was sorry I was sick; he understood and said that he had already removed the rental request and the booking fee as well. My marriage was saved, and I couldn't wait for James to get back with his coffee so I could share the good news.

My excessive talking also included excessive emailing, and I emailed the property owner a note of thanks. I then wrote, "Your actions seemed Christian-like. Are you a Christian?"

He replied, "Yes, very much so! I am so happy you asked! Jesus is my everything. I presume you are as well. COVID-19 has really got me shook up. I feel like we are staring at end-time events here very shortly."

By the time my husband returned with his coffee, I had developed a bond with the property owner. In our later conversations, I revealed that I was going to write a book about my journey. He said that his mother had attempted to write a Christian book and had lost $25,000 in the process. He said he would help me publish my book because he might have some "business sense." This never came to fruition, but I am grateful to him; he was an angel in disguise.

I told my husband that our credit card was cleared of the charges and everything was OK, but he realized I wasn't well and called our doctor. James explained my symptoms to Dr. Lavine, who diagnosed it as mania, for which the prescription was sleep. He outlined a plan to help me, with melatonin and an early bedtime, and he asked that I shut off my cell phone by 9:00 p.m.

Within one week of this process, I was on the road to recovery. On our trip to Florida, I visited the mansion and met the wonderful man who forgave my bad decision. It was a lovely home, and I am forever grateful for kind people in this world.

> The Lord replied, "My Presence will go with you, and
> I will give you rest." (Exodus 33:14)

Live life large. Thank God for everything. If you can sleep at night, thank Him.

ASKING FOR HELP

During our battle with COVID-19, many people asked how they could help. Our food ran low after several days of quarantining, but we didn't want to impose. Our local grocery stores and food delivery services didn't deliver to our area. A saint in our building bought us Gatorade, water, and sherbet, and another one brought us a home-cooked meal. They left them on our doorstep, and we were so grateful. Neither James nor I was accustomed to asking for help; we were too prideful.

Pride is a mighty tool of Satan, possibly his favorite weapon against Christians. We believe that we have it all together, are in control, and are capable of taking care of everything, but COVID-19 made us both very sick, and none of that was so. My children offered to bring food, but we declined their offers. Finally, when my niece called and asked if she could have prepared meals sent from Harry and David's, I reluctantly accepted. She discovered they didn't deliver to our area so she immediately called my son and said we needed food. He bought us so much food that he had to wheel it to our door with a dolly. We were so grateful, and I learned a valuable lesson— accept offers to help; it blesses you and blesses the giver. After I recovered, several people in our condominium said they would have helped us with shopping, food preparation, dog care, or anything else, had they known we were quarantined. From this experience, I began a meal-preparation plan for those in need in our building.

In the hospital, I was too weak to walk and had to ask for help to get to the bathroom. This was a very humbling experience. I wore a gaping hospital gown, was connected to oxygen and intravenous fluids, and was lying in a prone position. I teetered on the bedside until an aide or nurse was able to don all of the protective gear. I dreaded pushing the help button each time I needed it.

For several years, Pastor Fulton led our previous church. He's an amazing, gentle, humble, and knowledgeable man, whom I deeply respect. I struggled with a Bible verse to close one of the chapters in this book, and I called to request his help. I learned a valuable lesson during my COVID-19 journey: *ask for help*. He offered several applicable verses, but before he hung up, he asked me if I remembered my first experience with him.

He said it was his first day at work in the office, and I had come in to see the office manager, my dear friend Sophia, before I went out to deliver some flyers for a program that I wanted to start, Parents' Day Out. This was a program on Sunday mornings to which people could bring their children, and I would babysit their little ones while they shopped, dined out, or just took a break from child-rearing. I wanted to teach children Bible verses, sing songs, and help them learn of Jesus's love for them so they would be better prepared to grow up in this world. I'd hoped I could change one little life.

I had my flyers in hand and was headed to Starbucks, grocery stores, day care centers, or any other place that would let me post them. I stuck my head in his office door and said, "Pastor Fulton, are you on the clock yet? I wanted you to pray for me as I go out to post these flyers."

He laughed and said, "Yes, I am on the clock"—I guess pastors are always on the clock—and he laughed about it again.

I had no recollection of that comment, but I do remember I made him laugh. You never know what you will say, positive or negative, that will stick in another person's memory.

I remember my father saying to me, "Is that your nose or a

banana you are eating?" and "You should sue the city for building the sidewalks too close to your behind!" The comments held an element of truth—my nose isn't perfect, and I am short. He was trying to make me and anyone within earshot laugh, but I remember those and other negative comments he made, and they will stay with me for life.

"Here comes one of my favorite people. How are you today?" Pastor Fulton said as I walked into church one Sunday.

"Are you being sarcastic?" I asked.

"No, I meant that," he said, sounding shocked that I would question his sincerity.

One day, as I left his office, he said, "Hey, now go and do what you do best."

I turned and asked, "What is that?"

"Go spread joy!" he answered.

I walked a little taller that day because his comment was positive and encouraging. Positive, uplifting, and helpful words build self-confidence and a sense of security. Speak them often so the following generations can live life large.

> Finally, brothers, whatever is true, whatever is noble, whatever is right, whatever is pure, whatever is lovely, whatever is admirable—if anything is excellent or praiseworthy—think about such things. (Philippians 4:8)

Live life large. Asking for help is not a sign of weakness. It is putting aside pride and allowing people to use their God-given gifts to bless you, which ultimately blesses them.

DEATH

An email I received after I got out of the hospital wished me well and ended with the words, "I did hear that you are home and getting stronger. That is terrific news. I know several individuals who have not been so lucky. May your recovery continue."

I am very blessed; so many have died from this horrible disease, "the Beast." As of this writing, over two million people, worldwide, have died—a staggering loss of life.

Elaine, my sweet friend, lost her husband while I was in the hospital, not to COVID-19 but to cancer. I never know what to say to someone who has lost someone dear to them, but I know some people will experience the loss of a loved one to COVID-19, and the following texts we shared seems like a touching example of how to begin a dialogue.

Me: "Just a quick reach-out. I am in the Johns Hopkins Hospital with COVID-19. I am healing slowly. It was serious. Thinking of our friendship and you. Want to get together some day, when I am able."

Elaine: "I am so sorry. I want to hear more. Richard is in the hospital. Bad night."

Me: "Another blockage? Poor baby. I am so sorry, Elaine."

Elaine: "I am so sorry. If you are able, please tell me things like how/where do you think you got this? Anyone else in your family with it? How do you feel—specifically? You are the only person I know who has gotten this. Prayers surround you. We need you to get better. Much love to you."

Me: "James had it. I can't text too much. I can't walk two steps. We have both been quarantined 4 12 days!"

Elaine: "412 days? Has it been that long since we saw each other? Is James also at Hopkins? I love you. Get better, please."

Me: "No—for twelve days. James is home and out of quarantine. I have ten more quarantine days."

Elaine: "Get better, my sweet friend."

Me: "I love you."

Elaine: "Back at you my dear, sweet friend."

Two days later, Elaine's husband died.

Me: "Oh, my dear, precious, beautiful friend. My daughter just let me know of Richard going to wait for you up in heaven. He fought the good fight. He's free but that does zero to comfort you right now when you just want to hold him. I get that. I pray God's peace surrounds you in this dark place right now. Cry out to Him. I love you so much."

Elaine: "I love you too and was waiting until you felt a little better. Lousy time in my life right now but so happy and excited for Richard, as he is healed in the arms of Jesus."

Me: "Lifting you in prayers. Standing in the gap for you. Leaving Baltimore in about thirty minutes, heading home. You are loved."

Elaine: "Are you better?"

Me: "I am like a fragile little bird right now but better. We have something in common, but we serve a God big enough to deal with us both. He's got us, Elaine. Wish I could hold you right now, my sister. In time."

Elaine: "I love you too, sweet friend. I am anxious to hear your COVID story. Sleep well tonight."

Me: "You as well, my little bird friend. We will soar on wings like eagles. I promise you that."

Elaine: "Thank you. I will hold you to it. I need a motivator."

Me: "We all do at some point in our lives. I'm your girl."

Elaine: "My mom and sisters are whisking me away for a few days."

Me: "Oh good. Have so much fun. Enjoy every moment and know you are so loved by me and God."

Elaine: "Thank you—we are going to a quilt shop in Illinois."

Me: "Oh, what a comforting thought comes to mind when you say quilt—like chicken soup for the body, right?"

Elaine: "Yes, I am getting ready to make one for our bed. Going to sleep now—or trying to. Haven't been sleeping well."

Me: "Oh, fall into His loving embrace. He's waiting to hold His child in His arms. That's how He rolls."

I read in Charles Spurgeon's *Morning and Evening*,

> Angels waft thee away. Farewell, beloved one, thou art gone, thou wavest thine hand. Ah, now it is light. The pearly gates are open, the golden streets shine in the jasper light. We cover our eyes, but thou beholdest the unseen; adieu, brother, thou hast light at eventide, such as we have not yet.

> Where, O death, is your victory? Where, O death, is your sting? (1 Corinthians 15:55)

Live life large. We don't know when we will breathe our last breath, so live each moment you are given with purpose and direction from God.

LEGALISM

A᷆T The JHH, my doctor and I high-fived on sharing the same zodiac sign—Leo. There was a time when I would have said, "Oh, my goodness, I don't read my horoscope," but that now sounds pious and judgmental. God never gave us the job title of *judge*. In the Bible, it says, "Do not judge, or you too will be judged" (Matthew 7:1). I can name ten different things I have done on ten different days for which I don't want to be judged. Who am I to judge anyone?

During my hospital stay, God brought to mind a Bible verse in an interesting way. During my scariest and worst times, my valleys, God unfolded Micah 6:8. The first part began as I lay prone on my bed on the first day, and the Holy Spirit seemed to impress upon me, "He has showed you, O man, what is good. And what does the Lord require of you?" The remainder of the verse slowly unfolded as different incidents occurred. "To act justly" came after a very scary breathing episode; "to love mercy" after another breathing episode. And the last part of the verse came when they shut off the oxygen, and I was breathing on my own: "and to walk humbly with your God" completed the verse. God was working on me in an area that He knew I needed His help. Each section of that verse was indelibly written on my heart, mind, and spirit. There is no room for piety, judging, or self-righteousness. We are to love others, no exceptions. I feel I am not alone in my pharisaical attitude. It hasn't served me well, and from the declining attendance in churches, it has not served the church well either. I don't need to include statistics on church attendance, but I can tell you there were fifteen to twenty people in our church service on any Sunday. We had great pastors who preached great sermons. We fed the poor and helped with disaster relief efforts. We supported missionaries. Yet we must find another way to reach people and get them into Bible-believing churches. I believe it's one soul at a time. I love the saying, "They don't care how much you know until they know how much you care." I believe we need to love folks into the kingdom right in the middle of the messes in which they find themselves.

Just before we moved to the shore, our church, out of necessity of closing its doors, merged with another church. I was sorry I left because it was such a positive step in the right direction. The new pastor called me when he found out I was sick and said he was praying for me. He is such a caring, God-fearing man who loves his flock.

There are so many hurting people within a short distance of that church who have been turned off by organized religion. I wish I could tell each one that they would be so blessed to grow closer to Christ under this pastor's watchful care. I know they would feel the love he and his family exude.

After leaving the hospital and developing mania, I finally slept for a little while one night, and my first dream was that I ran to the pastor's car in the church parking lot to thank him for praying for me. Later, I called him and told him my dream, and he was so happy that I'd been blessed with deep sleep. There are so many amazing, loving pastors at Bible-believing churches. My prayer is that people will find a church home where they feel loved and accepted, and it will begin a lifelong journey to be the person God created them to be.

In the early 1990s, I worked in a large office building. Our offices were separated by low partitions, so we heard everything spoken in the adjoining cubicles. One Monday morning, my "partition partner," Ed, got a visitor who asked about his weekend.

Ed said, "It wasn't good because some religious folks knocked on my door, and when I answered, they waved a Bible in my face and said I was going to hell if I didn't believe in Jesus as my Lord and Savior."

"What was your response?" his guest asked.

"I was so frightened," Ed said, "that I shut the door in their faces."

I believe if this is how we think we can influence people for Jesus, like with Ed, it will miss the mark. I read of quite the opposite approach in *Jesus Calling* by Sarah Young: "Then you will be able to smile at people with My Joy and love them with My Love." I think this is how Jesus would reach people.

I heard part of a sermon that impressed me:

> Today, we are called to live a good life. James describes a good life as one where our deeds, our everyday actions, are done in a humility that comes from heavenly wisdom. We are to picture one who lives peacefully, doing good, and who has a gentle strength about them. They receive wisdom from above, which requires a listening spirit, seeking counsel from God as they maneuver the daily challenges of this world. (Pastor Sims's sermon on September 22, 2020, taken from James 3:13–17)

Brant Hansen wrote an amazing book, *Unoffendable.* I have read it many times and have recommended it to everyone I know because I believe this exemplifies Micah 6:8. Brant Hansen retells an incident that happened to Dr. Tony Compolo while he was traveling in Hawaii. Dr. Compolo couldn't sleep at 3:30 a.m., so he went to a local diner. While he ate a doughnut and drank coffee, the door opened, and eight or nine harlots came in and sat in the seats surrounding him. The one next to him, Agnes, said it was her thirty-ninth birthday the next day. The other girls sarcastically asked if she wanted a cake and a party. She answered, "I've never had one before; why start now?"

After they left, Dr. Compolo asked if the women came in every night at that time, and if so, could he throw a birthday party for Agnes? The diner owner and his wife said that Agnes was one of the nicest ladies in town, and they would help with the party too.

The next night, Dr. Compolo and the diner owners decorated the diner with a large sign that read, "Happy Birthday, Agnes," and they had a birthday cake. Word must have spread because by 3:30 a.m., the diner was filled with harlots. When Agnes walked in, everyone shouted, "HAPPY BIRTHDAY, AGNES" and they sang "Happy Birthday to You." Agnes was visibly shaken, and after she blew out the candles, she asked if she could take the cake home to show her mother.

Dr. Compolo said, "It's your cake. You can do with it as you wish."

She left, and the diner fell silent. Not knowing what to say, Dr. Compolo said, "Let's pray," and he prayed for Agnes. He prayed for her salvation, for her life to be changed, and that God would be good to her. When he opened his eyes, the diner owner was staring at him.

"I didn't know you were a preacher," he said, "What kind of church do you belong to?"

Dr. Compolo later said that the words came to him at just the right time as he responded, "A church that throws birthday parties for harlots at 3:30 in the morning."

The diner owner said, "No, you don't. There's no church like that. If there was, I'd join it. I'd join a church like that!"

Bret Hansen went on to write,

> You know what? I have a new rule: I won't join a
> church that doesn't do that. Because that's the Jesus

I recognize, the One who mends the brokenhearted
and is never, ever scandalized by sinners.

Tony Compolo said, "That is the kind of church Jesus came to
create on this earth, one that brings joy to those with no joy in their
lives."

For we are to God the aroma of Christ among those
who are being saved and those who are perishing. (2
Corinthians 2:15)

Live life large. "Sometimes our most powerful witness for Christ
comes as we just silently love those in front of us" (Jean Watson,
*Everything Can Change in Forty Days, A Journey of Transformation
through Christ*).

KANE BROWN

Kane Brown is one of my favorite singers; his music videos were instrumental in my journey. He reminds me of my son because he has the same type of arm-sleeve tattoo, and he resembles my son in build and hair color. I thought about the tattoos and the verse in the Old Testament, "Do not cut your bodies for the dead or put tattoo marks on yourselves, I am the Lord" (Leviticus 19:28). I struggle with many parts of the Law and question legalism.

In Charles Spurgeon's daily devotional *Morning and Evening*, he discusses a leper:

> [B]ut Jesus so far from chiding him broke through the law himself in order to meet him. He made an interchange with the leper, for while he cleansed him, he contracted by that touch a Levitical defilement.

There are other examples in the Bible of Jesus breaking the Law, such as healing on the Sabbath and talking to a woman living in sin:

> Then he said to the man, "Stretch out your hand." So he stretched it out and it was completely restored, just as sound as the other. (Matthew 12:13)

> "I have no husband," she replied. Jesus said to her, "You are right when you say you have no husband.

The fact is, you have had five husbands, and the man you now have is not your husband. What you have just said is quite true." (John 4:17–18)

Jesus loved the people more than he worried about keeping the Law.

Kane Brown had "John 3:16" tattooed on his chest. It was his first tattoo and is one of the most popular Bible verses used to reach the lost.

While I was in the hospital, I watched Kane Brown's music video *What Ifs* many times. Kane Brown and Lauren Alaina reminded me of my son and his wife, and I missed seeing my family. I would show the nurses and nurses' assistants the video when they came in my room and told them of the family resemblances. I thought about the many interesting facts of *What Ifs* while lying in bed, recovering. I have lived with a what-if mentality my entire life, and while in the hospital, I decided I didn't want to live like that anymore.

Kane Brown and Lauren Alaina exuded so much passion for life in that video. I think passion is beautiful and so important if you want to convince someone of something. I related it to telling others about Jesus and convincing them that He was so passionate toward them that He *died for them*, the epitome of passion.

I also noticed that Lauren Alaina was very comfortable in her own body, designed by God. She is beautiful, and I thought of the Bible verse, "I praise you because I am fearfully and wonderfully made; your works are wonderful, I know that full well" (Psalm 139:14).

I gleaned so many lessons from the song "What Ifs;" I hope everyone will watch the video and learn valuable lessons of their own on how to live life large. So many people live with a what-if mentality, and it has worsened with this pandemic. In Matthew, it asks, "Who of you by worrying can add a single hour to his life?" (Matthew 6:27).

So many people are worried about getting COVID-19, but it is exhausting to try to protect yourself and live in a bubble. I believe we can only do what the authorities say: wear a mask, wash your hands before touching your face or food, socially distance by six feet, and avoid crowds. People call me often to ask me to pray for their family members or friends who have been diagnosed with COVID-19, which I do. After experiencing COVID-19 myself, I can empathize with their needs. Now, as I go through my day, I imagine myself in a golden light ray, coming down from heaven. I try to live within the boundaries of that beam because I believe God only promises us that He will be present in the present moment. When my thoughts wander to yesterday's choices or tomorrow's worries, the ray dissipates, along with my peace.

When I was discharged from the hospital, I danced to Kane Brown and Marshmello's song "One Thing Right." It was perfect to help me regain balance, strength, and energy. More importantly, the lyrics reminded me of my relationship with Jesus.

> Jesus said to her, "I am the resurrection and the life.
> He who believes in me will live, even though he dies;
> and whoever lives and believes in me will never die.
> Do you believe this?" (John 11:25)

Live life large. Jesus came so that we could have not only eternal life but the abundant life in the here and now. Don't miss out on that by living in a what-if mode.

TREY KENNEDY

WHEN MY DAUGHTER HEARD I WAS GOING INTO THE HOSPITAL, she told me that if I couldn't sleep, I should watch old videos of Trey Kennedy. He is an amazing Christian comedian, and she and I are huge fans. We can't wait for his next video to come out so we can watch it and call each other to crack up together and share our favorite lines. He is so astute. He does an excellent job of acting out what "middle schoolers be like." My grandson is just getting through that stage, and it seems like Trey must have been in my grandson's home when he created those videos. He nailed my grandson's behavior; he truly did.

On the second night in the JHH, I had a dose of dexamethasone, and sleep was nowhere on my radar screen. At about 2:00 a.m., I remembered my daughter's advice. I searched for old videos by Trey Kennedy and found one titled *Driving with Your Girlfriend*, which I began to watch. I was on oxygen, lying in the prone position, and I didn't expect to almost trigger the oxygen alarm because of laughing hysterically, but that's what happened.

In the video, Trey Kennedy is driving, and his girlfriend thinks he almost hit a squirrel so she screams. I don't know why it affected me like it did, but I had to ask God to help me shut down that video because I laughed so hard that my oxygen levels dropped, and I began to panic. I couldn't get my breath, and I came close to knowing firsthand what it's like to die laughing.

I have no idea why this next part of my journey took place, but Trey Kennedy must have been on my mind when my manic state set in. I had watched most of his videos by the time I left the hospital. Frequently, he asks his fan base to provide ideas for his next video—ideas of their funny experiences or life incidents that he could weave into a skit. In my manic state, I was involved in a constant dialogue with a hallucination that I believed to be God. He said he wanted to use Trey Kennedy's support base to get out a message to the world, and I was to give him that message. The message made so much sense to me, and I agreed it was a perfect way to reach millennials and younger generations. Another symptom of my mania was that my mind raced at a hundred miles per hour, and I could think of so many things at once; the mind is quite phenomenal.

I was to create a whole video for Trey based on COVID-19, and because I had just survived it, I would be totally believable. I accepted the challenge immediately and included hilarious scenes about hospital gowns opening in the back, hospital food, hospital costs, waking up at all hours so the nurses could draw blood and take my vital statistics, and everything you can think of that's possibly laughable during a hospital stay. But the pièce de résistance was the last line; it was from "God" himself: "In all seriousness, people, you might get through COVID-19 with a two-week vacation from school or work. You might experience minor symptoms or maybe none at all, but when you go to crowded bars and packed pubs in high numbers, COVID-19 germs could cling to your hands, clothes, or hair, and you could transfer them to your older family members when you walk back into the house. You are like a petri dish of germs when you return from partying. If you want to be responsible for culling the entire older generation in your family, keep doing what you are doing and don't wear masks or wash your hands or stay six-feet apart from your friends."

This dialogue was so real to me. I knew, without a doubt, that God wrote the message and chose Trey Kennedy to deliver it to his fan base. I knew I had to get through to Trey. On the night I arrived home, I started texting him. I wrote the whole skit for him, sent it to him that evening, and then waited for his call.

No call came, so I texted again, telling him I knew his readers needed to hear this. "Just call me, and we can discuss it," I wrote.

In my mind, I began a dialogue of what I thought would transpire when Trey called me to discuss the "new video." It went something like this:

Trey: "Hi, this is Trey Kennedy. I bet you can't believe I'm calling you, right?"

Me: "No, this is great stuff and directly from God, so I was pretty sure you would call."

Trey: "This is so great. I will work on it immediately."

Me: "I thought so!"

Trey: "Hey, why don't you come out to Oklahoma to meet me, and we can discuss it?"

Me: "Ha-ha, me? Drive? Well, after COVID-19, I'm certainly not getting into an airplane, but drive to Oklahoma just to meet Trey Kennedy? Do you have, like, the biggest potato or the biggest ball of string or even a small museum or anything else of interest? Because if not, then it's probably not happening."

Well, that cracked me up, and I thought he would find that really funny.

No call from Trey.

Then I texted him about his obligation to God—to put this out and warn people. Still no response.

It was getting really late, and I started quoting the Bible to him through another text. I told him he was acting just like Jonah, and he had a message to deliver to the younger generation (Nineveh). "Go to the great city of Nineveh and preach against it, because its wickedness has come up before me" (Jonah 1:2). But, I told him, he was running in the opposite direction (Tarshish). "But Jonah ran away from the Lord and headed for Tarshish. He went down to

Joppa where he found a ship bound for that port. After paying the fare, he went aboard and sailed for Tarshish to flee from the Lord" (Jonah 1:3).

Still no response.

Then I texted him: "OK, I am going off the grid, and you won't be able to talk to me about the upcoming new video. You have ten minutes to respond."

Still no response.

I gave him ten minutes more, and then I shut off my phone for the night, thinking, *It's OK. He'll call tomorrow for sure.*

As all of this transpired, James pleaded with me, "Stop texting him. It's getting weird. You are stalking him."

I dismissed his comments.

The next day, there still was no call from Trey Kennedy or his staff; he never called me and didn't use my message from "God." Of course, I know now that it wasn't from God because if it had been, His message would have been delivered. It was, however, the first sign of mania, but I didn't recognize it.

I did use Trey Kennedy's comedy to get me through the hospital stay, and it lightened up a very dark time in my journey. I am grateful for his ministry.

> A cheerful heart is good medicine, but a crushed spirit
> dries up the bones. (Proverbs 17:22)

Live life large. "Do Less, God Bless"—that's the title of Trey Kennedy's podcast.

MAX

EARLIER THIS YEAR, WE MOVED FROM A SINGLE-FAMILY HOME with a quarter-acre fenced-in yard to a two-bedroom, fourth-floor condominium—seventy-five steps up. In our previous home, our dog rang bells we attached to the doorknob to let us know he needed to go outside to take care of business. We all enjoyed that arrangement.

One day, pre-COVID-19, I said to my husband, "What if we both got sick at the same time and neither of us could walk Max?"

"What are the odds that we'd both become sick at the same time?" he asked.

"Quite low," I said.

We had two rescue cats before Max came to live with us, and they ruled the house, but when Max appeared, their roaming days ended. Max was twelve weeks old and had been in several shelters before he came to live with us. He was delivered to us from his final shelter in Tennessee, and from that day forward, life changed drastically for the cats. He is a mixed breed but must have some hunting instincts because anything that moves is fair game to him, including cats. One day, I had to pry one of the cats from his mouth; he'd almost killed her. Over the last five years, we have placed a gate at our bedroom door to separate the pets; the only solution is to keep them apart.

Then COVID-19 *did* affect both of us at the same time. We discussed our dog and his walking needs with our county health department contact. She said of course we had to walk him, and it was OK to go out for his bathroom breaks. But I was so sick and weak that I couldn't help at all with his care. He stayed on my bed and barely left my side as I continued to decline.

James had a high fever and terrible cough, but he pushed himself to take Max outside as often as possible, going up and down those seventy-five steps. James was getting worse but wouldn't use the elevator for fear of infecting others. The steps were more open, and he wore a mask and gloves and took disinfecting wipes to clean every surface he touched.

One night, Max got sick at one thirty and had to go outside. James got up, took him down the steps, and stayed outside in the damp night air for about twenty minutes. They climbed back up the steps after Max had eaten enough grass to settle his stomach. After that incident, I knew we would have to find a place to take Max the next day. I thought we would have to surrender him to the local shelter—I'm sure other COVID-19 victims had to experience that loss. I am so sorry for them because I know what it is like to love a dog.

I called a local kennel and asked if they would take a dog from a COVID-19 family. I know the woman could hear the sadness in my plea for help. She said, "Bring him over. Of course we'll take him."

I cried. I called her "Mrs. Angel" from that day forward.

She said she'd disinfect him and all of his belongings and keep him for as long as we needed. I packed some dog food and sent his blanket, but that was all I could do. I was too weak to care and had no choice but to let him go.

My daughter made me laugh when she said he might be nicer to the cats when he came home because he'd think that was why he was sent away. I pictured him between the two cats with a fake smile on his face.

When he left, I thought he'd be there for only a few days, but then I had to be hospitalized. From the hospital room one day, I called and talked with "Mr. Angel." I had no idea what their names were but Mr. and Mrs. Angel seemed quite fitting. I told him I was in the hospital, quite sick, and I asked about Max.

He said, "I'd like to tell you that Max is curled up in a fetal position and almost dead because he misses you so much, but he's barking and running with a Great Dane, and earlier today, he ran with the little dogs. He's very happy and believes he's in charge of the whole kennel."

I was so relieved to hear this news.

Then he told me, "At night, before I turn off the lights, I look at Max and say, 'You know she'd pick you up if she could.' Max looks up at me with his big, soulful brown eyes, sighs, and puts his head on his paws, as if he understands perfectly."

I thought that when I got out of the hospital, we could pick him up immediately from the kennel, but James and I were still too weak to walk him. Days turned into weeks, and we would plan to pick him up, but when the scheduled day approached, we realized we were still too weak to handle him.

I called one day and said, "Mr. Angel, I bet you are almost out of his dog food, so I will have it shipped to you."

He laughed. "We ran out of his food quite a while ago. Max has been eating the same food as all the other dogs in his kennel. He's fine."

"*What?*" I cried. "*Regular* dog food?" I laugh about this, but we are now feeding him that same food and saving monthly on his food bill.

Max was in the kennel for twenty-one days before I felt we could care for him. James had to return to work, and I was trying to regain strength.

The day we picked him up, I got the following text from a friend:

> If I were Max, I'd expect extra servings at dinner
> for the next year at least! He did not sign up for this

neglect. If he knew what he knows now, he says he would've stayed in Tennessee! So give the fella some slack if he seems cold and distant when you first meet up. And please, bring a gift!

When Mr. Angel brought Max out, I thought he'd jump all over me and knock me down, but he greeted me with quiet reserve.

Mr. Angel said, "Dogs have no concept of time. He doesn't know it's been twenty-one days since he's seen you." He told me a story of a State Department employee who had to leave her dog for a one-week business trip while she traveled out of the country. The trip turned into a year, and she had to leave her dog in the kennel. I didn't feel quite so bad after hearing that story.

A friend sent me a get-well card that read, "Whoever said that diamonds are a girl's best friend … never owned a dog."

There have been some changes since Max has been home. I decided that I am in charge, and he's the dog. He is no longer an idol, and we are working on getting him to respect the cats and my commands. We are in a good place now, and everyone is happier.

> A righteous man cares for the needs of his animal.
> (Proverbs 12:10a)

Live life large. Can't we all just get along?

ELLEN DEGENERES

WHILE I WAS IN THE HOSPITAL, I TOLD MY DOCTOR I WAS going to write a book about my journey through COVID-19.

"When it hits the *New York Times* best-seller list, I want the first signed copy," she said.

I didn't think of her comment again until I was home and diagnosed with mania. Sleepless nights, a racing mind, and a vivid imagination had become the norm.

James asked me many times, "To whom are you talking in the middle of the night?"

"I was rehearsing lines for a TV show," I told him.

As usual, he shook his head and prayed for me to return to normal.

To pass the late-night hours, I would make up skits for *The Ellen DeGeneres Show*, speaking her lines and mine. Some of the lines were so funny that I would laugh hysterically while my husband tried to sleep. My family once told me that I had a lot in common with Ellen. We had the same short haircut and about the same eye color, and we both danced and made people laugh.

I thought about all the similarities with one difference and said, "She's a lesbian, and I am straight."

In one of my imagined skits, Ellen said, "You are a Christian. How do you feel about homosexuality?"

One of my favorite singers is Lauren Daigle. Soon after I got out of the hospital, my cousin Addie texted me:

> Listening to Lauren Daigle as I clean and the song "I Am Yours" came on, and it made me think of you! Look up lyrics. Powerful! Hope you're doing well. Love you!

When Lauren Daigle was asked that same question during an interview on the *Domenick Nati Show* on iHeart radio, she answered as I would have:

> In a sense, I have too many people that I love that they are homosexual. I don't know. I actually had a conversation with someone last night about it. I can't say one way or the other. I'm not God. So when people ask questions like that … that's what my go to is. I just say read the Bible and find out for yourself. And when you find out let me know, because I'm learning too.

My Sunday school teacher offered his opinion on Lauren Daigle's response, saying, "That is the best answer she could have given."

I played in a women's golf league with a woman who was gay. She was also a lawyer for the US Department of Justice, very quick-witted, funny, encouraging, and a wonderful person. I never told her that her lifestyle was wrong, and she didn't ask me. I would have told her the same thing, though: "Read the Bible and find out for yourself."

In my imagined role on *The Ellen DeGeneres Show*, I said, "Let's not talk about homosexuality exclusively. Let's talk about senseless murder, substance abuse, abortion, adultery, child pornography, human trafficking, and a lot of what we see happening in our world. What is the answer? I believe the answer is a personal relationship with Jesus. I believe that if you acknowledge that He is who He says He is, the Holy Spirit will enter into your heart, and you will want to live your life pleasing Him and following His Word, the Bible."

At this point in her show, I fell out of my chair backwards. I'll explain why.

Around my neck I wore a Tiffany's necklace with a small oval tag. "Ellen," I said, "tell them why I fell out of my seat!"

When she looked befuddled because I was making this up, I said, "Come on, Ellen; tell the audience what is going on." She looked like a deer caught in headlights, so I said, "OK, I will tell them about your warning system."

I proceeded to tell the audience, "Ellen gave me this necklace to wear, and it is actually a shock system, similar to a dog's shock collar. She has a button under her desk that she dials in numbers from one to ten—number one delivers a very small current but all the way up to ten which knocks the guest over backward. Then Ellen ends the interview and calls in her security staff to escort the person out because he or she is incapacitated."

When I answered her questions with noncontroversial remarks, I didn't feel a thing, but if I approached a subject that would decrease her TV ratings, I felt a small shock. Throughout the program, I had been jumping slightly and grabbing the tag on the necklace, but after the last discussion, I was carried out by security.

This made me laugh; it was just close enough to reality to not make me question how sick I was in this manic mode.

Another imagined monologue concerned the number of TV sets in Ellen and Portia's home. I'd seen pictures of their home, and I said, "You probably have about eight big-screen TVs in that mansion, right?"

She said, "About."

I said, "I've seen a homeless shelter in your town. You should donate one of those TVs. I'll bet they all crowd into a small room with a small TV, and they have to watch the TV show that the biggest and strongest bully wants to watch. I imagine a newcomer to the group might say, 'Hey, is there a chance we could watch *The Ellen DeGeneres Show* today?' and all of the others turn to see who had the audacity to ask such a silly question. The bully replies in his deep, gruff voice, 'No way, man! We want to watch a good show that makes us laugh, *The Adventures of Rocky and Bullwinkle and Friends*!' Ellen, if you could just donate one of those TV sets, this wouldn't happen. Let's face it; you and Portia together only have four eyes. Four eyes for eight large-screen TVs? Do the math; it doesn't work. Please donate a TV for them."

This made Ellen laugh, and she had just taken a drink of her water, which she spewed all over my arm. I jumped up with exaggerated disgust and said, "Ellen, we are in the middle of a major pandemic, and you are going to spew spit all over me? My people will be in touch with your people, and we'll see if we can settle this out of court."

The audience laughed. And I laughed so hard that I shook the bed, and my husband woke up—*again.*

I went into this much detail because it was 100 percent clear in my mind that this entire scenario would transpire sometime in the future. It was at this point, though, that James asked me to sleep in the guest room until the mania subsided. He had no idea with whom I was talking and laughing at three in the morning. My mind was working overtime, and I was having a great time, writing an episode for Ellen's show. She and I played off each other beautifully, although I was playing both roles. The scary thing was that in my mind, it was working beautifully. I had the entire lineup of guests—Lauren Daigle, Trey Kennedy, Kane Brown and Lauren Alaina, and all of my family. This was so believable in my mind that the next day, I called my son and told him not to be surprised if one day he and Kane Brown were comparing tattoos on a TV show. I had no idea that this was abnormal behavior. I just thought I was very talented and very funny.

There is a time for everything, and a season for every activity under heaven: … a time to weep and a time to laugh. (Ecclesiastes 3:1, 4a)

Live life large. Laughter is a gift from God. Laugh as often as possible; it's great for body, mind, and spirit.

CATHERINE

I MET CATHERINE WHEN WE MOVED TO THE SHORE. SHE LIVED IN our condominium. Catherine fell and broke her hip several months before we met and was struggling to walk. She shuffled along and walked very carefully and slowly.

When James and I returned from sailing one afternoon, I told him that we needed groceries. Catherine was outside and overheard our conversation. She asked if she could go with me to the grocery store.

I glanced at James apprehensively. I knew I could run in and run out of the store in my normal, type A, rush-rush demeanor (before COVID-19), and I suspected she would slow me down.

She picked up on my hesitation and said, "I can go some other time."

My husband gave me one of those "what kind of person are you?" glances, and I quickly did an about-face and invited her.

After we parked at the local store and taking what seemed like an hour to get to the front door, she got her cart, and we separated to shop. In about ten minutes, I placed my cartful of items on the conveyor belt, paid, and waited, somewhat impatiently, in the front of the store. No Catherine. I called her phone about three times and then texted her, but she didn't respond. I was about to have her paged, but then I saw her. She had a couple of items in her cart and had beads of sweat on her forehead. She looked as if she was hurrying to avoid keeping me waiting. I am sure I switched my weight from one foot to the other as I leaned on my cart and gave the impression of an impatient woman who had to attend a function for which she was being detained.

The truth was that I had nowhere to be, no one to meet, and no time clock to punch; I was just comfortable in my hurried lifestyle and unaccustomed to slowing down.

Catherine and I became good friends after that and have gone many places and done many things, but I can't help but see the difference between us. I cringe every time I think about it.

When I was diagnosed with COVID-19, I had to tell a few people in our condominium. Catherine was one of them because I had been with her shortly after I was exposed. I suggested she get tested too. When I went into quarantine, Catherine checked on me often. When the ambulance took me to the hospital, Catherine left me a voice message on my phone: "An ambulance just pulled away. Please tell me you aren't in it." Catherine was crying.

I was weak when I was taken to the hospital but nowhere near the shape in which I came home. I was shocked that a very healthy, spirited, energetic woman who walked her dog many times a day and climbed seventy-five steps three times a day could be left in such a weakened state. I questioned whether I could get out of the cab when I arrived home and was afraid that I couldn't walk to the elevator without passing out. I again had to pray for Jesus to take my hand and help me. And then, there was my friend Catherine. She brought me a delicious dinner for my first evening home; she had worked very hard to prepare a feast to welcome me home.

I stayed in bed for many days and was able to get up only for a minute or two before I became exhausted and out of breath. After being bedridden for a week, James said I needed to get outside and walk around our little square that we use as a dog park. It is the size of a small backyard with a sidewalk around it, but I didn't think I could make one lap. I asked Catherine to go with me in case anything happened. I took my utility cart and met her outside, where we proceeded to shuffle around the loop together. I later learned people were looking out of their windows and wondering what had happened to the lady who, earlier that month, had been power-walking with her dog. But Catherine was encouraging, and we looked like twins, except I was moving slower than she was now.

Then it happened. I was about to get schooled in walking a mile in someone else's shoes. I had to go to the grocery store two weeks after I came home from the hospital, and Catherine said she would take me. You can probably see the writing on the wall. She drove, and I had serious doubts whether I could walk to the front door of the store. She held up traffic so I could cross the parking lot, and I was exhausted before I got into the store with my cart. My breathing was labored, my heart was pounding, and I needed to rest before I could put anything into my cart.

Catherine stopped with me, and she helped me. As I struggled to get my few groceries onto the conveyor belt, I saw that Catherine was finished. She was in the Starbucks line, ordering a coffee and *patiently* waiting for me to finish. Oh dear, had the tables turned. At that point, I felt how she felt before I got sick. It was a very hard lesson for me.

One day, I said my feet were cold, and I didn't have any slippers. Within the hour, she was knocking on my door, a beautiful pair of turquoise slippers in hand that she didn't need.

A billboard flashed before my eyes that read, "Until you have walked in someone else's shoes, you have no idea how they feel."

A friend loves at all times, and a brother is born for adversity. (Proverbs 17:17)

Live life large. God didn't create us to live life at such a pace that we lose track of what really matters—love and friendship.

RACE

Race riots prevailed in the United States when I was diagnosed with COVID-19. People fought, burned cities, and toppled statues. The hatred was so evident among black and white Americans; angry faces and mob scenes dominated the newscasts. The hospital seemed impervious to the daily news. I prayed aloud with everyone who came into my room; color made no difference.

I am more comfortable praying in public since I left the hospital. When I regained strength, I walked Max past our bridge tender, who had opened and closed our creek's drawbridge for our sailboat's mast most of the summer. I wanted to put a face to the voice and make the bridge tender some snacks as a thank-you for helping us. I knocked on the door of the shack and out popped Amanda, a long-time bridge tender, a black American.

Cars passed by as we discussed my COVID-19 diagnosis, recent hospital stay, and her fears of contracting the disease. I sensed her uneasiness about being around me. She said paranoia had crept into her life. I prayed with everyone I met, so it seemed natural to ask Amanda if she would like to pray together. And there, right on a busy bridge, she and I bowed our heads, and I prayed for her safety and my continued healing.

I had stopped by to thank the unknown tender for her service but left with a newfound friend. I invited her to come to my church and worship with me that Sunday, but she didn't want to be around other people during the pandemic.

As I waited for a prescription in the local drugstore, a black American woman introduced herself, and we began to talk. She was limping, and I asked her if I could pray with her for her pain; she agreed. Again, in public, a black American and a white American, heads bowed, serving the same Lord, prayed together. I invited her to come to my church and worship with me that Sunday.

A prayer trailer was set up outside our local grocery store. A black American pastor with a megaphone prayed for people as they drove by and was available for people to stop by and pray in his mobile chapel. After shopping one day, I felt the Holy Spirit nudge me to stop and ask him for prayer—for my healing, my family, this book, and this torn country. We prayed, and he offered a most beautiful, heartfelt prayer.

I placed my white arm against his black arm before I left and said, "Look at this—black and white, together, praying. We are different, but we are really the same, created by God in His image."

He said, "If they cut you and they cut me, we would bleed the same color onto the ground. We are the same."

We talked about current events, and I asked him why the world was in the state it was.

He said, "Satan is rearing his head and trying his best to divide everyone. He knows he's lost the war, but he's doing everything he can to keep the battle alive and divide everyone."

I have stopped by his prayer trailer since that time to pray and support his street-corner ministry. He is a fantastic preacher and a powerful prayer partner.

Several years ago, our church had a live manger scene for Christmas. Members of the congregation dressed as Mary and Joseph and shepherds. I was Mary, and the shepherds tended live sheep. Our church by the side of the road stood close to a very busy intersection. It was visible to all who passed by on that Christmas Eve, even in the dark, with misty rain. Late that night, the sheep were returned to their stalls, and all of the characters went home to prepare for Christmas, except me. I held a baby doll wrapped in a blanket and, dressed in the garb of that day, held the baby near the manger. I stayed because I thought, *If one person, in their busyness, looks over and sees me standing in the spotlight, holding a baby, their heart might be touched, and Christmas will become real to them.* My prayer out there on that chilly night was, "Make Jesus real to them."

My prayer for the people driving over the bridge, shopping in the drugstore, and driving by the mobile prayer trailer was the same: "Red and yellow, black and white, they're all precious in His sight" (C. Herbert Woolston, "Jesus Loves the Little Children").

As I wrote this chapter, I was sitting on a rooftop balcony in inner-city Baltimore on a beautiful, crisp fall morning. The bright sun warmed me, and as I looked out, my eye caught a church with three towers, each topped with a simple cross—the Father, the Son, and the Holy Spirit. I stopped in awe to thank a very loving Savior, and I prayed for peace in our land. I prayed that that peace could be felt by those who were hurt, unloved, rejected, and hopeless. I so wished they knew my Jesus; I believe He is the only answer.

Our gym closed at the beginning of the pandemic. Two other women, both black Americans, and I have formed an accountability group to perform planks every morning at eight thirty to maintain core strength. We talk frankly about race issues.

I said, "I'm sorry for what happened to your people years ago. I was sickened by the treatment of slaves that I read about in Frederick Douglass's book *Narrative of the Life of Frederick Douglass, an American Slave.*

One of the women said, "You know that everything happens for a reason."

The other said, "Everything is orderly, and this hate will only stop one person at a time."

I don't know what it was like to grow up as a black American, but I think empathy would be a welcome change to ignorance. I pray that God will change hearts and lives, one at a time, in this great country that we share.

> Let us therefore make every effort to do what leads
> to peace and to mutual edification. (Romans 14:19)

Live life large. No matter your generation, you can love as Jesus loved: red and yellow, black and white .

PRAYER WARRIOR

I COACHED AT A WOMEN'S GYM FOR MANY YEARS. WHEN THE women found out that I'd tested positive for COVID-19, they reached out in love, prayers, and concern. Theresa, an author and wonderful woman of faith, had lost about eighty pounds and had kept it off for many years. She also survived stage-four pancreatic cancer, after the doctors told her there was nothing more they could do for her. One day after a workout, she gave me a small book, *The Power of a Praying Grandparent* by Stormie Omartian. She had no idea that she'd been used by God and how important her gift was to me. That afternoon, my daughter called and asked for much-needed prayer for one of my grandchildren.

I took out my copy of *The Power of a Praying Grandparent* and wrote in it: "An unbelievable miracle on the day I needed it most. But God. To God be the glory. Great things He hath done." Since that day, I have prayed two prayers a day from that book for all my grandchildren.

When I was in physical therapy for a knee injury, I took the book with me to pray. One of the technicians saw the book title and poured out her story of a beloved grandchild in trouble. I told her I'd pray for him; when I got home, I ordered a copy of the book and gave it to her at the next session. She was grateful.

We are put on this earth to help people in their time of need, and sometimes, only God knows their time of need. We must be quiet enough to hear His still, small voice and be obedient to follow His leading.

Theresa also gave me a journal for a Christmas gift. Written on the cover is, "She Who Kneels Before God Can Stand Before Anyone." Theresa wrote on the cover page:

> We are therefore Christ's ambassadors, as though God were making his appeal through us. (2 Corinthians 5:20a)

God knew about my journey and that I would be at this place, at this time, and write a book that would let Him speak through me, which was my prayer on the day my journey began at the wildlife refuge. *But God*—isn't He amazing?

Theresa also wrote, "Wherever you are, whatever you do, before you even say a word, let them know that you belong to the Lord."

When I came home from the hospital and couldn't sleep, I wrote the majority of this book from 11:00 p.m. to 5:00 a.m. It was written so hastily that most of the words were illegible. I questioned whether I was supposed to write this book or whether this was something I had imagined too. I became disheartened as I tried to decipher the writings—page after page of scribbles and abbreviated words. Satan put "FEAR" into me—False Expectations Appearing Real. I called Theresa and asked her to pray with me because I couldn't read my writing. She and I prayed but she also uploaded a special prayer to YouTube, where I was able to see her angelic face and hear her beautiful, special words of encouragement.

If you are socially distanced, isolated, or quarantined, don't hesitate to take advantage of modern technology to pray for family, friends, and loved ones. I want to share her words.

> Hi, this is Theresa. I wanted to be faithful to send you a message of encouragement this morning about your writing. I pray that you will be strong and courageous.

In the Bible, Joshua had to take over for Moses (and those were big shoes to fill). Yet God came and told him, through Moses, to be strong and courageous, *strong and courageous.* And our strength is not from ourselves, just like the talents and the gifts that we have; they're really God-given. And I was actually thinking about the fishes and the loaves today and that God gives us quite a lot, and we can do what we want with them, but they have the potential of feeding so many more people when we remember to give it to Jesus first. So, my prayer is that *that* is how you will start every writing session, that you will remember that your gift belongs to the Lord. And if you allow Him to bless it, it will be a blessing to so many more people. But let me pray right now. "Father, in the name of the Lord, Jesus Christ, I thank you for capturing our hearts. I thank you that we belong to You. I pray, Father, for this gift that You have given her, this story that has happened to her, this miracle that You have worked in her life. I thank you, Father, for protecting her life, but more importantly, Lord, I thank you that she belongs to You. She is a woman of God; help her never to forget that. I pray, Lord, to never forget that, in the name of Jesus, I pray. Amen." Have a wonderful day of writing. You know God is with you. He's right beside you. Take care. God bless you. *Open that book.*

Therefore confess your sins to each other and pray for each other so that you may be healed. The prayer of a righteous man is powerful and effective. (James 5:16a)

Live life large. Surround yourself with God-fearing friends. Call on them when you need prayer, and be there for them when they do.

HELENE

MY CHILDREN'S GRANDMOTHER IS OKINAWAN, A HERITAGE OF which they are very proud. She gave us a beautiful silk scarf that she had worn as a young woman that depicts people walking over a bridge somewhere in Asia. We framed it and have treasured the only piece of her childhood we knew. Helene is ninety-four, and all of our requests to learn about her past had been met with excuses and refusals to provide details into her early life.

When I was on bedrest after my hospital stay, I had many free hours to talk with people. As I've mentioned, mania symptoms put my mind into overdrive, and one day, she and I held an information exchange that equaled no other. With pen in hand, I donned my reporter's cap, realizing this information might be lost forever if I didn't record it. Sometimes it is difficult to understand my mother-in-law, but during our session, she was clear and animated—what a gift for our family and for her as well as she shared story after story. My questions flowed naturally from her responses, and we talked comfortably about her past for the first time in over forty years. I learned so much. Don't miss an opportunity to get a glimpse into the past of your loved ones.

This is her story. Helene lived in Okinawa in a large house with a barn that housed cows, sheep, and two pigs per year. Her family never took a vacation or left the house because all the animals had to be fed. They butchered two pigs, once a year, which provided their meat. They preserved the meat in salt, and all the cuts resembled bacon. They never ate fish because her mother hated the smell. They had a big garden but not at the house; they had to walk to get there. They sold the animals in town, and that's how they made their money. They never had a pet dog or cat, only farm animals.

Her father, a carpenter, borrowed money from the townspeople to build their house. Every month, her family prepared a meal for the money lenders until Helene's father slowly paid them back. In the kitchen of their house, on a clay floor, stood a wood stove, where her mother prepared their meals. The family ate in a large room off of the kitchen; sliding glass doors separated the rooms. The main house had wooden floors covered with rice mats. Their bathroom was in the barn with the animals, and they had a well by their house where she fetched water in a bucket. She slept in a bedroom with her mother.

The seasons changed but not drastically. There was no snow, and it never really got cold, but Helene was prepared with winter clothes, if needed.

The youngest of four children, Helene was the only girl and was spoiled by her parents and treated "very nicely" by her older brothers. Some of her favorite times were spent with her family at the beach behind their house. It was a very short walk, and once they crossed the railroad tracks, they were there. Catching shrimp during shrimp season was most memorable, even though Helene was too young to hold the net. The moon phase determined shrimp season, she remembered, and her mother walked backward through the water, dragging the net, because shrimp swim backward. They cooked and ate the shrimp for dinner after a fun day at the beach.

Helene was a tomboy, and while her many friends played with dolls (they'd make a little house out of tree limbs and leaves), she would climb trees because that was her favorite thing to do. She thought her friends were "silly" for playing with dolls, and she wanted no part of that! One day, Helene and a friend visited her maternal grandmother's house and stole oranges off the trees. Her grandmother ran after them, but Helene said her grandmother could never catch them as they were "very fast, young girls."

That grandmother didn't like Helene. She put wire around the lower branches of the orange trees so Helene couldn't pick the oranges. Helene wasn't particularly fond of her grandmother either. She told Helene that she was a "mean kid" because she stole peanuts, oranges, and sugar cane. Helene loved to squeeze the juice out of the sugar cane.

Helene's uncle had a lot of property and raised sugar cane. Horses pulled some type of cutting device to harvest the cane. They boiled the sugar cane and made brown sugar, but it was too dangerous for her to be near the heat. She remembered, vividly, a narrow food-storage area behind her grandparents' house where they stored many jars of raw peanuts, peas, and salted meats.

Helene's paternal grandparents were from different classes of people and spoke different languages. Her grandfather married her grandmother despite their class difference. They grew bananas, green oranges, and peaches.

Helene's large house was confiscated when the Japanese occupied Okinawa. She remembers seeing one star on the Japanese officer's uniform who took over their house. Her family moved to a much smaller house, while the one-star officer lived alone in their house. Two of her brothers were captured by the Japanese. One was forced to work in a factory, making airplane parts; the other was made into a soldier because, Helene said, "That's what they did with all of the eighteen- and nineteen-year-old boys."

The oldest brother went to the Philippines because he heard he could make a lot of money there, but he never returned; she thinks he was killed. Helene's father begged her brothers not to go back to the Philippines because they were losing the war, but the youngest brother went anyway, against her father's wishes. Her father didn't think he'd come home alive.

Everything changed in Okinawa when the Japanese took over.

Helene's school was occupied so her classes had to meet outside, forcing her to study in the grass. She was taught Japanese in school but had forgotten most of it. Helene was required to speak Japanese in school but was often caught speaking Okinawan. The punishment for this infraction was having a string with a tag on it taped on your head or your neck. The punishment was meant to shame the children, but Helene didn't care; she spoke Okinawan anyway and had many tags put on her. (She thought that was funny and laughed at this part of the story.) She attended school until the seventh grade but then had to take over home duties with her family. Her job was to cut the grass with a machete, a tool so sharp "you could cut off your finger."

Every year, they attended a celebration in her town to honor the fishermen who fished in small canoes, not big boats. The celebration was like an open-air market, where you could buy clothing and all kinds of things. It had a "big party atmosphere." She always enjoyed attending.

She said that her father lived to be about a hundred, but she wasn't sure because it was very disrespectful to ask your parents their ages. She had no idea at what age her mother died.

Her parents spoke Okinawan when they were at home.

She had a paternal uncle who was a "big shot" in the community. She couldn't remember his title but he collected taxes. She said, "He told people how much they had to pay. He was very smart and elected to his position." One day, however, he was sent to the Philippines, and she never saw him again.

Another paternal uncle was sickly—"very pale and white." She thought he had heart trouble, and he couldn't do much. He hanged himself because he was sick so often. One of her maternal uncles, a "very, very rich" farmland owner, raised cows and would come back from auctions with "wads of money."

"The war destroyed everything," she reminisced sadly. "Okinawa was a beautiful place."

Helene met Michael, her husband, a US Air Force civilian stationed in Okinawa, in the Officers' Club when American soldiers occupied the Island. She said they had "so much fun dating in Okinawa." She remembered that the mess hall workers picked some type of small, sweet berries by climbing steps to the mess hall's second floor, reaching out windows, and pulling off whole tree branches to pick the berries. She supposed they didn't really care about the trees, but she certainly enjoyed those berries.

Helene and Michael later flew to the Philippines to be married, and their first son was born there. They were then transferred to Tachikawa, Japan, where their second son was born. Helene remembered she was able to walk off base very easily in Tachikawa, and she would frequently go out to buy tofu. They always had housekeepers, so they must have had enough money. She said she'd love to see Tachikawa again, but she probably wouldn't be able to understand the Japanese language.

They then went from Japan to an air force base in California because "service people just went where they were told to go." Helene remembered a "most romantic time" when Michael had been gone for a week with a five-star general. Michael wasn't a pilot but was heavily involved with airplanes. When he returned, she saw him get off the plane and said that he looked "so handsome." He had blond hair and blue eyes, was quite tall, and looked "very good" in his khaki uniform. What she most remembered—which she described with a softness in her voice that I'd never heard—was, "He was so happy to see me. He missed me so much that week; he was so much in love with me." He had to quit flying shortly after that because he suffered from earaches when he reached certain altitudes.

I found it so interesting, listening to her memories. She played them back like movie scenes, and I was blessed to be the audience.

Remember the days of old; consider the generations long past. Ask your father and he will tell you, your elders, and they will explain to you. (Deuteronomy 32:7)

Live life large. Please don't let the older generations leave this world without giving them an opportunity to share their stories.

SMOKING AND VAPING

TWO NEAR-DEATH RESPIRATORY EXPERIENCES IN THE HOSPITAL made me realize I never want to die that way. They also made me realize that I don't want *anyone* to die that way so I took it upon myself to sound the alarm. I called my son to tell him that he almost lost his mother. I told him I'd like to warn his father, a smoker, about the scariness of not being able to breathe. Here's what I wanted to say to him:

> What can I say to you that would convince you to never want to be where I am right now? To be unable to breathe is horrible. Please stop smoking, just because you want to enjoy some time with our newest grandchild. It will be worth it to see our son get some payback for his antics through which he put us. He would so want her to know you. Please stop, for the grandkids. Good night from the Infectious Diseases Unit.

Most people don't want to be told how to live their lives, but I thought my having acute respiratory distress syndrome (ARDS) gave me license to warn everyone about the dangers of smoking and vaping. After all, I reasoned, horror stories are written about being buried alive and running out of air. I knew what it was like to be unable to breathe, and I knew what it was like to try to quit smoking, as I too had smoked for a few years, forty years ago. I figured I was now qualified to become a no-smoking poster child.

Katherine J. Wu wrote in the *New York Times* on September 4, 2020:

> Since the start of the pandemic, experts have warned that the coronavirus—a respiratory pathogen—most likely capitalizes on the scarred lungs of smokers and vapers. Doctors and researchers are now starting to pinpoint the ways in which smoking and vaping seem to enhance the virus's ability to spread from person to person, infiltrate the lungs and spark some of COVID-19's worst symptoms. "I have no doubt in saying that smoking and vaping could put people at increased risk of poor outcomes from COVID-19," said Dr. Stephanie Lovinsky-Desir, a pediatric pulmonologist at Columbia University. "It is quite clear that smoking and vaping are bad for the lungs, and the predominant symptoms of COVID are respiratory. Those two things are going to be bad in combination."

At the wildlife refuge, I met an artist who was in town for an art show. When he lit a cigarette in front of me, I took it upon myself to share my experience with COVID-19 and breathing difficulties. When I said I had just been released from the hospital, his first reaction was to step away from me. I told him how anxious I felt when I was not able to breathe, and he asked me to pray for him to stop the habit. Our paths will probably never cross again, but every morning, I pray for him to quit.

I read a story about a young boy who was walking along the beach, throwing starfish back into the ocean that had washed up on the shore.

A man asked him why he was bothering to do this. "So many are dying on the beach," he told the boy, "it won't make a difference."

The little boy continued to throw the starfish back into the sea, one at a time, responding, "It makes a difference to that one."

I have included this chapter because maybe one person will kick the habit, and it will make a difference to that one.

> Blessed is the man who finds wisdom, the man who gains understanding, for she is more profitable than silver and yields better returns than gold. (Proverbs 3:13–14)

Live life large. Learn from the adage, "You can lead a horse to water, but you can't make him drink." Warn others, but don't get upset if they don't change. Sometimes a person has to experience something firsthand to benefit from the impact.

COUSIN BRIAN

MY COUSIN BRIAN IS AN OUTDOORSMAN. HE IS HAPPIEST WHEN he is hunting, playing tennis, making fires, driving boats, and participating in any other outdoor activity. Last fall, Brian borrowed a friend's tree stand to hunt very early one morning. The ladder's top rung broke, and he fell about fifteen feet to the ground, shattering his right hip joint. He incurred several other injuries to his face and hands as he grazed the tree trunk as he fell. Brian has a high pain threshold, but he knew that this accident was bad. His cell phone fell out of reach, and he couldn't move. The only way he could attract attention was his alarm on his car keys, which were in his hip pocket. He struggled against unbelievable pain and was able to push the alarm.

Two Good Samaritans arrived and called the EMS. They helicoptered him to a hospital in Virginia that specialized in shock trauma. Our family soon rallied around him with prayers, visits, food, and support. The hospital stay and rehabilitation translated into months of hard work and downtime for Brian.

So many strong-faithed men and women were praying for me—family, friends, pastors, church prayer chains, and foreign missionaries. They stormed the heavens on my behalf and stood in the gap when I couldn't. I will always be grateful to all of them.

Brian texted me when I was in the worst stages of COVID-19 and said, "I talked to Jesus this morning about you, and I might have shed a tear." That meant so much to me, and I still cry when I remember his words. The humbleness of that short text touched a place deep in my soul. Another day, he told me that when he was alone in the early morning hours, watching the sunrise in the woods, he prayed to Jesus, "Don't take her yet"—a simple prayer, yet one I will never forget.

Brian has a house on a lake in Gettysburg, Pennsylvania. I spent many weekends and vacations on that lake because my parents also owned a house on that lake. My children have many fond memories of growing up there, but one of the fondest is our evening boat rides. About an hour before sunset, my dad would gather me, my mom, my kids, and our dog, and we'd go for a beautiful, peaceful boat ride around the lake before turning in for the night. It was a way of closing out the day. Each ride would begin with Dad asking Mom to "put on the coffee" so that he and I could sip our coffee in the sunset during our ride.

My son has fond memories of these rides because he was able to sit on his pop's lap and drive the boat. My daughter recently texted me a picture of her pop driving the boat with our dog, a beautiful yellow Labrador retriever, sitting on the back seat with a contented look on her face. These rides were treasured by our family.

Brian just bought a new power boat that trumps all of the boats we have ever owned, a Malibu Response. He called me one day when I was in the hospital and told me that when I was ready, I could drive his boat, full speed, down the lake. Brian *lives life large*, and he offered me an opportunity to join him. I couldn't wait to get out of the hospital and feel well enough to take him up on his offer. It took many, many weeks, but I did. He and I took a boat ride, complete with a coffee cup to toast my late dad.

At Brian's insistence, I put the cup down and gave that Malibu's powerful engine full throttle and drove that boat faster than I have ever driven. What a day it was, finished with steaks on an open-fire pit. I won't forget that day.

Brian told me that he and his wife were driving about one hundred miles to walk in the Franklin Graham Prayer March 2020 through Washington, DC, the next weekend. I feel he is growing into a very usable vessel for the Lord. I am grateful that my cousin loves me.

> And without faith it is impossible to please God, because anyone who comes to him must believe that he exists and that he rewards those who earnestly seek him. (Hebrews 11:6)

Life life large. Don't let fear or busyness deprive you of enjoying life to the fullest. Jesus came to give us abundant life on this earth. Enjoy every day.

DRAGONFLIES AND DAMSELFLIES

Wˣˣᴇᴎ I ᴏʀɪɢɪɴᴀʟʟʏ ɢᴏᴛ ᴛʜᴇ ɪᴅᴇᴀ ᴛᴏ ᴡʀɪᴛᴇ ᴀ ʙᴏᴏᴋ, ᴛʜᴇ title was *The Emerald-Green and Black Dragonfly: One Patient's Journey through COVID-19.* I envisioned the front cover of the book—very simple, black and white, with a strikingly beautiful dragonfly sitting on my T-shirt on the cover. I contacted my friend Lauren, an artist, and she and I looked for pictures that she could use to draw this beautiful insect. As we texted pictures back and forth, it dawned on me that it wasn't a dragonfly at all—but what was it? So as any normal "Google-holic" would ask, I did a search for "What looks like a dragonfly but isn't?" My answer came back: "A damselfly." These insects are closely related and are both in the Odonata order. There are two major groups of Odonata: dragonflies and damselflies, which I didn't know until I ordered a great book by Dennis Paulson, *Dragonflies & Damselflies: A Natural History,* first published in the United States and Canada in 2019, by Princeton University Press, Princeton, New Jersey. On Page 19, I read:

> The hard exoskeleton of odonates lends itself to being shiny and metallic. Jewelwings/demoiselles (Calopterygidae) and emeralds (Corduliidae) are among the most metallic, especially some of the former, with entirely brilliant green or blue bodies.

I considered myself so blessed to have witnessed a part of God's creation—His brilliant green-metallic masterpiece.

My cousin forwarded me an article from Nature.com, "Dragonfly Wings Might Save Lives." It was interesting; it related to all of the COVID-19 germ horror stories that I'd heard over the last eight or nine months. But I realized the article related to *bacterial* germs, and COVID-19 is caused by a *virus*. The article on Nature.com was based on a 2020 article from Springer Nature publishing company, titled "Antibacterial Effects of Nanopillar Surfaces Are Mediated by Cell Impedance, Penetration and Induction of Oxidative Stress" (J. Jenkins et al., "Antibacterial Effects ...," *Nature Communications* (April 2, 2020). The wings of dragonflies and damselflies are *nanopillars* (nanoprotrusions), and they have been found to rupture bacteria on contact. I read that scientists are studying the surface structure of those wings to create synthetic surfaces in surgeries, on common surfaces (e.g., door handles, bathrooms, elevators), and on artificial limbs.

I include this information because I am touched by the enormity and brilliance of the God we serve. He designed a beautiful insect that I saw for less than a minute and enabled intelligent scientists to study their wings and emulate that surface to break up bacteria. I hope you are as impressed as I am by this breakthrough. I mentioned it to a doctor who was excited about the much-needed nanoprotrusion-surface discovery for surgery rooms.

I sent the following text to Lauren:

> It was the most amazing thing I have ever witnessed in sixty-eight years—really, the most beautiful thing I have ever seen created by God. ... I have been truly blessed to have laid my eyes on this insect. I am set for life as far as miracles go!

God saw all that he had made, and it was very good. And there was evening, and there was morning—the sixth day. (Genesis 1:31)

Live life large. If you are quiet and still in His presence, maybe He will show you too a jewel from His majestic creation.

SANCTUARY ROOM

THE DAY MY JOURNEY BEGAN AT THE WILDLIFE REFUGE, I ASKED God to help me make James my top priority. He had dropped too far down the list, behind children, work, dog, exercise, and many other things over the years. Little did I know that within ten days, I would be hospitalized and have many hours to contemplate changes I could make to put "feet" on that prayer.

Parts of this journey were quite dark to me, and I wanted nothing physical surrounding me that was reminiscent of that darkness. In the hospital, I envisioned decorating with sea-glass colors, with white and light-gray walls replacing the existing darker colors. I wanted to paint the existing black furniture white. I wanted a "sanctuary" to which James and I could escape the world and all of its distractions and share peaceful moments to love each other.

My hospital visit reiterated that I should not put off simple pleasures; life is about the little things. This lesson began before my journey when we listed our home for sale. Our savvy real estate agent convinced us to make many changes in our house, which was a wise decision, as it sold quickly. We repainted it in beautiful designer-gray shades; refinished all the hardwood floors; installed new kitchen appliances and matching countertops; added impressive lighting; manicured the landscaping; and created a house we hardly recognized but immediately loved. The irony of this is that for twenty-five years, we had lived with mediocrity when we could have enjoyed these upgrades, changes, and enhancements while we lived there. Before we closed the door for the final time, we had a family dinner, with Chinese carry-out on paper plates, to say goodbye to our home and close a chapter in our family's life. Parting was such sweet sorrow, and we vowed we wouldn't wait twenty-five years to make changes to our new home when we moved to our two-bedroom condominium on the shore. If we could afford it, we would create living spaces that filled us with joy—spaces to which we loved to come home.

The theme of this book is live life large, and I believe that it's important to add joy and happiness to your life wherever you are able. Sometimes, this is done spontaneously. After I'd returned from the hospital, I walked into the kitchen one morning and didn't see any of the food my son had brought us—my husband had put it away, as I was too weak to stand. So many surprises appeared as I recuperated.

My appetite and sense of taste slowly returned, and when I opened the pantry, I saw a box of milk-chocolate-covered pecans. My inner reasonable self said, *You can't eat chocolate -covered pecans at 5:30 a.m.!*

Hmmm, why not? asked that live-life-large self, brought to life by this disease. *Do you think an alarm will sound if you eat some chocolate-covered pecans before breakfast? Will you ruin your appetite? Will your mother find out and call from Florida to yell at you? What could possibly happen to you except that the delicious chocolate will melt in your mouth, and you will enjoy the contrast of the crunchy pecan?*

I removed the lid and ate several of those yummy chocolate-covered pecans. And guess what? No alarm sounded, I still ate breakfast, and Mom didn't call me on the phone to yell at me for eating sweets before breakfast.

> This is the day the Lord has made, let us rejoice and be glad in it. (Psalm 118:24)

Live life large. Your life can change in a minute. Don't put off doing something that brings you joy.

THE JOURNEY ENDS

I DROVE BACK TO THE WILDLIFE REFUGE WHEN I REGAINED MY strength. It was a perfect eighty-degree day with a brilliant-blue, cloudless sky. I sat in the same spot where my journey had begun. I was deep in prayer, thanking God for my journey and the truths He had showed me. I saw a few dragonflies but not the emerald-green and black damselfly that had landed on me what seemed an eternity ago.

A man and his small son arrived and started a conversation with me, which became about damselflies—he was quite knowledgeable.

"If you want any chance of seeing a damselfly," he said, "you'll have to venture into the woods. I saw them hunting mosquitoes."

As he turned to leave, I read a tattoo on his leg: *Be the change you wish to see in the world*. As I thought about those words, I also thought about the changes I'd requested God to help me make on day one of my journey.

The stark realization hit me that, one day, James and Max would both die. But after my journey, I didn't believe I would ever be alone. God was so real to me on day one, as I sat on the pier in the marsh; so real throughout my entire COVID-19 journey. Now, He was still making Himself known in the solitude of the moment, speaking lovingly and quietly to my heart.

The Lord is gracious and righteous, our God is full of compassion. The Lord protects the simple hearted; when I was in great need, he saved me. Be at rest once more, O my soul, for the Lord has been good to you. For you, O Lord, have delivered my soul from death, my eyes from tears, my feet from stumbling, that I may walk before the lord in the land of the living. (Psalm 116:5–9)

Live life large.

He has showed you, O man, what is good. And what does the Lord require of you? To act justly and to love mercy and to walk humbly with your God. (Micah 6:8)

That's it. That's what He requires.

Printed in the United States
by Baker & Taylor Publisher Services